Study Guide to accompany

SOCIOLOGY

in our times

the essentials

First Canadian Edition

Diana Kendall
Baylor University

Rick Linden
University of Manitoba

Jane Lothian Murray
University of Winnipeg

Diane Symbaluk
Grant MacEwan Community College

I(T)P Nelson

an International Thomson Publishing company

Toronto • Albany • Bonn • Boston • Cincinnati • Detroit • London • Madrid • Melbourne
Mexico City • New York • Pacific Grove • Paris • San Francisco • Singapore • Tokyo • Washington

I(T)P® **International Thomson Publishing**
The ITP logo is a trademark under licence
www.thomson.com

Published in 1998 by
I(T)P® Nelson
A division of Thomson Canada Limited
1120 Birchmount Road
Scarborough, Ontario M1K 5G4
www.nelson.com

ISBN 0-17-616641-6

Publisher and Team Leader	Michael Young
Acquisitions Editor	Shirley Tessier
Production Coordinator	Brad Horning
Cover Design	Angela Cluer

Printed and bound in Canada
3 4 (WC) 01 00

TABLE OF CONTENTS

Preface

This study guide is designed to help the reader identify and learn the key terms, people, and issues contained in each of the chapters in Kendall, Lothian Murray, and Linden's (1998) *Sociology In Our Times: The Essentials*. For each chapter in the textbook, the following sections are provided: a chapter outline, a brief chapter summary, a list of key terms, a review of key terms, a list of key people, a review of key people, a list of learning objectives, and a set of learning objective tests.

The chapter outline provides topic headings and indicates materials covered in a given chapter. A brief chapter summary highlights key issues. The list of key terms identifies major sociological concepts while the review of key terms provides definitions of the key terms. A list of key people indicates the theorists and researchers who contribute to the topics covered in the chapter. The review of key people lists the major contributions of these individuals. The learning objectives identify majoy issues and indicate what a student is expected to learn by the end of the chapter. Learning objective tests quiz the reader on the key issues, terms, and theorists covered in the chapter through the use of multiple choice, true-false, fill-in-the-blanks, and matching items.

The following instructions are suggestions for using this guide:

1. Read over the chapter outline to familiarize yourself with the materials covered.

2. Skim over the chapter summary and then read that chapter in the textbook.

3. Expand on the chapter summary by taking notes and use the outline for headings.

4. Write out a definition for each of the key terms and include examples.

5. After studying the definitions, complete the review of key terms.

6. Write out the list of key people, indicating the major contribution of each person.

7. Test your knowledge by completing the review of key people.

8. List the learning objectives and provide detailed answers to these items.

9. After reviewing the chapter and your notes, complete the learning objective tests.

10. Check your answers with those provided and review items you had difficulty with.

CHAPTER 1
THE SOCIOLOGICAL PERSPECTIVE: THEORY AND METHODS

Chapter Outline

Chapter Summary

Sociology is the systematic study of human society and social interaction. Sociology enables us to see how individual behaviour is largely shaped by the groups to which we belong and the **society** in which we live. Some early social thinkers, including **Auguste Comte, Harriet Martineau, Herbert Spencer,** and **Emile Durkheim,** emphasized social order and stability; others, including **Karl Marx,** and **Max Weber,** focused on conflict and social change. Sociologists use three primary theoretical perspectives to examine social life: (1) **functionalist perspectives** assume that society is a stable, orderly system; (2) **conflict perspectives** assume that society is a continuous power struggle among competing groups, often based on **class, race, ethnicity,** or **gender;** and (3) **interactionist perspectives** focus on how people make sense of their everyday social interactions. Sociologists conduct research to gain a more accurate understanding of society. Sociological research is based on an **empirical approach** that answers questions through a direct, systematic collection and analysis of data. **Research methods** are systematic techniques for conducting research that include **experiments, surveys, analyses of existing data, participant observation, complete observation, case studies, and ethnography.** Many sociologists use multiple methods in order to gain a wider scope of data and points of view. Studying human behaviour raises important ethical issues for sociologists.

Key Terms

anomie (p. 13)
alienation (p. 14)
bourgeoisie (p. 13)
case study (p. 33)
class (p. 10)
class conflict (p. 13)
commonsense knowledge (p. 5)
complete observation (p. 32)
conflict perspectives (p. 16)
control group (p. 28)
correlation (p. 29)
descriptive studies (p. 23)
developed nations (p. 7)
developing nations (p. 7)
dysfunctions (p. 25)
empirical approach (p. 45)
ethnicity (p. 10)
ethnography (p. 33)
experiment (p. 28)
experimental group (p. 28)
explanatory studies (p. 23)
functionalist perspectives (p. 15)
gender (p. 11)
global interdependence (p. 4)
industrialization (p. 10)
interactionist perspectives (p. 18)
interview (p. 30)
latent functions (p. 16)
macrolevel analysis (p. 17)
manifest functions (p. 16)

normative approach (p. 21)
means of production (p. 13)
microlevel analysis (p. 17)
objective (p. 5)
participant observation (p. 33)
perspective (p. 15)
power elite (p. 17)
proletariat (p. 14)
qualitative research (p. 23)
quantitative research (p. 23)
questionnaire (p. 30)
race (p. 10)
reliability (p. 26)
representative sample (p. 26)
research methods (p. 28)
respondents (p. 30)
sample (p. 26)
secondary analysis (p. 31)
sex (p. 10)
social facts (p. 13)
societal consensus (p. 15)
society (p. 4)
sociological imagination (p. 7)
sociology (p. 4)
survey (p. 30)
symbol (p. 18)
theory (p. 15)
urbanization (p. 11)
validity (p. 26)
variable (p. 25)

Review of Key Terms

_____ 1.	A set of logically interrelated statements that attempts to describe, explain, and predict events.
_____ 2.	The systematic study of human society and social interaction.
_____ 3.	Intended functions that are recognized by the participants in a social unit.
_____ 4.	Are based on the assumption that society is a stable, orderly system.
_____ 5.	Specifies groups of people on the basis of physical characteristics.
_____ 6.	A data collection encounter in which a researcher asks the respondent questions.

_____ 7. Exists when two variables are associated more frequently than could be expected by chance.

_____ 8. Strategies or techniques for systematically conducting research.

_____ 9. A condition in which social control becomes ineffective as a result of the loss of shared values and a sense of purpose in society.

_____ 10. Biological and anatomical differences between males and females.

_____ 11. A relationship in which the lives of all people are closely intertwined and any one nation's problems are part of a larger global problem.

_____ 12. Those who own and control the means of production.

_____ 13. The meanings, beliefs, and practices associated with sex differences.

_____ 14. Unintended functions that are hidden and remain unacknowledged by participants.

_____ 15. The struggle between the capitalist and working classes.

_____ 16. Free from distorting biases.

_____ 17. Tools, land, factories, and money that forms the economic basis of a society.

_____ 18. Cultural heritage based on language or country of origin.

_____ 19. A small clique of top corporate, political, and military officials.

_____ 20. A situation in which the majority shares a common set of values, beliefs, and behavioural expectations.

_____ 21. An overall approach or viewpoint on some subject matter.

_____ 22. Patterned ways of acting, thinking, and feeling that exist outside of any one individual but that exert social control over each person.

_____ 23. A large social grouping that shares the same geographical territory and is subject to the same political authority and dominant cultural expectations.

_____ 24. The relative location of a person or group within a larger society, based on wealth, power, or prestige.

_____ 25. Anything that meaningfully represents something else.

_____ 26. Focus on how people act toward one another and how they make sense of those interactions.

_____ 27. The ability to see the relationship between individual experiences and the larger society.

_____ 28. A poll in which the researcher gathers facts or attempts to determine the relationship between facts.

_____ 29. The goal is scientific objectivity, and the focus is on data that can be measured numerically.

_____ 30. Interpretive description rather than statistics is used to analyze underlying meanings and patterns of social relationships.

_____ 31. A printed research instrument containing a series of items to which subjects respond.

_____ 32. Focuses on small groups rather than large-scale structures.

_____ 33. The undesirable consequences of any element of a society.

_____ 34. A feeling of powerlessness and estrangement from other people and from oneself.

_____ 35. The process by which an increasing proportion of a population lives in cities.

_____ 36. An approach based on the belief that groups are engaged in a continuous power struggle for the control of scarce resources.

_____ 37. Any concept with measurable traits or characteristics that can change from one person, time, situation, or society to another.

_____ 38. Beliefs that guide ordinary conduct in everyday life.

_____ 39. The process by which societies are transformed from dependence on agriculture and handmade products to an emphasis on manufacturing and related industries.

_____ 40. A method in which the researcher systematically observes a social process but does not take part in it.

_____ 41. A carefully designed situation in which the researcher studies the impact of certain variables on subjects' attitudes or behaviour.

_____ 42. Experimental subjects who are not exposed to the independent variable.

_____ 43. Attempts to answer questions through systematic collection and analysis of data.

_____ 44. The extent to which a study or research instrument yields consistent results when applied to different individuals or the same people over time.

_____ 45. Those who sell their labour as their only means to earn a living.

_____ 46. Examines whole societies, large-scale social structures, and social systems.

_____ 47. The extent to which a study or research instrument accurately measures what it is supposed to measure.

_____ 48. Uses religion, customs, habits, traditions, and law to answer important questions.

_____ 49. A selection from a larger population that has the essential characteristics of the total population.

_____ 50. Attempt to explain cause-and-effect relationships and to provide information on why certain events do or do not occur.

_____ 51. Contains the subjects who are exposed to an independent variable.

_____ 52. Persons who provide data for analysis through interviews or questionnaires.

_____ 53. Attempt to describe social reality or provide facts about some group, practice, or event.

_____ 54. A detailed study of the life and activities of a group of people by researchers who may live with the group over a period of years.

_____ 55. A method in which researchers use existing material and analyze data originally collected by others.

_____ 56. Collecting systematic observations while being part of the activities of the group being studied.

_____ 57. Countries with highly industrialized economies.

_____ 58. Countries undergoing transformation from agrarian to industrial societies.

_____ 59. An in-depth, multi-faceted investigation of a single event, person, or social grouping.

_____ 60. People who are selected from the population to be studied.

Key People

Silvia Canetto (p. 27)

Auguste Comte (p. 11)

Ralf Dahrendorf (p. 17)

Emile Durkheim (p. 13)

David Karp and William Yoels (p. 32)

Harriet Martineau (p. 12)

Karl Marx (p. 13)

C. Wright Mills (p. 17)

Robert K. Merton (p. 16)

Talcott Parsons (p. 15)

Anastasia Shkilnyk (p. 33)

Herbert Spencer (p. 12)

Max Weber (p. 14)

Review of Key People

_____ 1. Set forth the idea that societies are built on social facts.

_____ 2. Described sociological reasoning as the sociological imagination.

_____ 3. Used an evolutionary perspective to explain social order and change.

_____ 4. Translated Comte's work and explored the status of women, children, and "sufferers."

_____ 5. A functionalist who claimed that all societies must make provisions for meeting social needs in order to survive.

_____ 6. Evaluated the role of the Protestant Reformation in producing a social climate in which capitalism could exist and flourish.

_____ 7. Believed that conflict—especially class conflict—was necessary to produce societal change.

_____ 8. Coined the term "sociology."

_____ 9. Distinguished between manifest and latent functions.

_____ 10. Observed that conflict is inherent in all authority relationships.

_____ 11. This person's research was based on a desire to find answers to the human destruction and suffering witnessed among the Ojibwa living in Grassy Narrows.

_____ 12. Conducted a complete observation study on student participation in university classrooms.

_____ 13. Used a qualitative approach in the study of suicide.

Learning Objectives

After reading Chapter 1, the student should be able to:

1. define sociology and identify some of the benefits of studying sociology (pp. 4-7).

2. explain what C. Wright Mills meant by "sociological imagination" and explain its importance in understanding people's behaviour (pp. 7-10).

3. define race, ethnicity, class, sex, and gender (p. 10).

4. identify Auguste Comte, Harriet Martineau, and Herbert Spencer, and explain their unique contributions to sociology (pp. 11-13).

5. contrast Emile Durkheim's and Karl Marx's perspectives on society and social conflict (pp. 13-14).

6. explain how Durkheim's notions of "social facts" and "anomie" contribute to our understanding of society (p. 13).

7. state the major assumptions of functionalist perspectives and identify the major contributors to functional approaches (pp. 15-16).

8. be able to distinguish between manifest functions, latent functions, and dysfunctions (p. 16).

9. state the major assumptions of conflict perspectives and identify the key contributors (pp. 16-17).

10. distinguish between microlevel and macrolevel analyses and state which level of analysis is utilized by the functional, conflict, and interactionist perspectives (p. 17).

11. state the key assumptions of the interactionist perspective (pp. 17-18).

12. compare normative and empirical approaches to examining social issues (pp. 21-23).

13. describe descriptive and explanatory studies (p. 23).

14. differentiate between qualitative and quantitative research and give examples of each (p. 23).

15. explain why validity and reliability are important considerations in sociological research (p. 26).

16. contrast experimental and control groups and explain why control groups are necessary in experiments (p. 28).

17. describe the major types of surveys (pp. 30-31).

18. define secondary analysis (p. 31).

19. describe the major methods of field research and indicate when researchers are most likely to utilize each of them (pp. 32-33).

20. describe the major ethical concerns in sociological research (pp. 33-35).

Learning Objective Tests

Multiple Choice Questions

1. Who translated and condensed Auguste Comte's work to make it more accessible to a wide variety of scholars?
   a. Emile Durkheim
   b. Harriet Martineau
   c. Herbert Spencer
   d. Jane Addams

2. Who claimed that society needed change because the majority of people are oppressed by a few wealthy individuals?
   a. Karl Marx
   b. Emile Durkheim
   c. Georg Simmel
   d. Herbert Spencer

3. Which of the following is NOT a key reason why we study sociology?
   a. Sociology enables us to see how acts such as sexual assault are personal problems.
   b. Sociology helps us gain a better understanding of ourselves.
   c. Sociology helps us gain a better understanding of our social world.
   d. Sociology enables us to see how behaviour is largely shaped by the groups to which we belong.

4. Interactionist perspectives focus on:
    a. macrolevel analysis.
    b. class conflict.
    c. social facts.
    d. shared meanings.

5. Conflict perspectives examine all of the following EXCEPT:
    a. exploitation.
    b. racial-ethnic inequalities
    c. consensus.
    d. patriarchy.

6. C. Wright Mills used the term "sociological imagination" to refer to:
    a. distorting subjective biases.
    b. knowledge that guides ordinary conduct in everyday life.
    c. a relationship in which the lives of all people are closely intertwined and any one nation's problems are part of a larger global problem.
    d. the ability to see the relationship between individual experiences and the larger society.

7. Which of the following statements is FALSE?
    a. Ethnicity is determined by wealth, power, prestige, or other valued resources.
    b. There are no "pure" races.
    c. Sex refers to biological differences between males and females.
    d. Masculinity and femininity are gender categories.

8. According to Emile Durkheim, a breakdown in traditional values and authority patterns will result in:
    a. patriarchy.
    b. group consciousness.
    c. societal consensus.
    d. anomie.

9. _____ perspectives assume that society is a stable system characterized by common values and beliefs.
    a. Conflict
    b. Functional
    c. Interactionist
    d. Feminist

10. Which of the following perspectives is examined using a macrolevel of analysis?
    a. functional
    b. conflict
    c. interactionist
    d. a and b

11. The transmission of knowledge and skills from one generation to the next is an example of a:
    a. dysfunction of education.
    b. manifest function of education.
    c. latent function of education.
    d. symbolic function of education.

12. With quantitative research, the focus is on:
    a. data that can be measured numerically, through the use of statistical techniques.
    b. interpretive description of words used to examine social relationships.
    c. Verstehen, or a value-free approach to the study of human behaviour.
    d. gathering data in natural settings and examining the information subjectively.

13. Which sociological approach is referred to as the scientific method in its attempt to answer questions through systematic collective analysis of data?
    a. normative
    b. empirical
    c. inductive
    d. deductive

14. What type of study is likely to report on census data or try to determine the number of people who recently contemplated suicide?
    a. descriptive
    b. explanatory
    c. experimental
    d. unstructured

15. A recurring issue in studies that analyze the relationship between religious beliefs and suicide is whether "church membership" is an accurate indicator of a person's religious beliefs. This example demonstrates which problem in research?
    a. objectivity
    b. sampling errors
    c. validity
    d. reliability

16. Observation, case studies, and ethnography are techniques used to obtain data using which form of research?
    a. experimental
    b. field
    c. survey
    d. secondary data analysis

17. What type of survey technique involves an interviewer who asks respondents questions and records their answers?
    a. questionnaire
    b. self-administered survey
    c. interview
    d. unobtrusive

18. If you were interested in finding out how much violence is contained in children's television shows, you would most likely adopt which method of research?
    a. experiment
    b. survey
    c. secondary analysis
    d. ethnography

19. Which of the following examples would be considered unethical in sociological research?
    a. The researcher was careful not to reveal information that would embarrass the participants in the study.
    b. Participants in an experiment consisted of students who were in the study as part of their course requirements.
    c. Students filling out teacher evaluations were told not to put their names or any identifying information on the forms they filled out.
    d. Participants in an experiment were told that the exercise they were about to perform had a slight risk of physical injury.

20. In an experiment, the group of people who participate in the study but are not exposed to the independent variable represent:
    a. the experimental group.
    b. the independent condition.
    c. the dependent condition.
    d. the control group.

True–False Statements

TF 1. Many commonsense notions are actually myths (p. 5).

TF 2. Karl Marx believed that societies were stable and held together shared moral beliefs (p. 13).

TF 3. According to interactionist perspectives, groups in society are engaged in a continuous power struggle for control of scarce resources (pp. 17-18).

TF 4. All feminist approaches share the belief that women and men are equal (p. 17).

TF   5.   Conflict perspectives assume that society is a stable, orderly system (pp. 16-17).

TF   6.   The normative approach is based on strong beliefs about what is right and wrong and what ought to be in society (p. 21).

TF   7.   Reliability concerns the extent to which an instrument measures what it is supposed to (p. 26).

TF   8.   Drawing a conclusion and reporting findings is the last stage in the sociological research process (p. 27).

TF   9.   Interviews are costly but effective in dealing with complicated issues (p. 31).

TF   10. Field researchers use methods that generate quantitative data (p. 32).

Fill-in-the-Blanks

1.   _____ helps us gain a better understanding of ourselves and our social world (p. 4).

2.   According to _____ perspectives, groups in society are engaged in a continuous power struggle for control of scarce resources (p. 16).

3.   Weber recognized the importance of economic conditions in producing inequality and conflict but added _____ and _____ as other sources of inequality (p. 16).

4.   From a functionalist perspective, society is a stable system characterized by _____ _____ whereby the majority shares a common set of values (p. 15).

5.   Sociologist C. Wright Mills (1959) described sociological reasoning as the _____ _____ (p. 7).

6.   A _____ analysis examines whole societies, large-scale social structures, and social systems instead of looking at important social dynamics in an individual's life (p. 17).

7.   _____ is an approach that is similar to participant observation but takes place over much longer periods of time (p. 33).

8.   The _____ _____ is based on the assumption that knowledge is best gained by direct, systematic observation (p. 23).

9.   A _____ exists when two variables are associated more frequently than could be expected by chance (p. 29).

10.   Researchers frequently select a _____ _____ from a larger population to answer questions about their attitudes, opinions, or behaviour (p. 26).

Matching Items

<u>1. Match the concept with the appropriate theoretical perspective.</u>

___ (a) social inequality   1. functionalist perspective
___ (b) societal consensus   2. conflict perspective
___ (c) subjective reality   3. interactionist perspective

<u>2. Match the concept with its originator.</u>

___ (a) alienation   1. Robert K. Merton
___ (b) social fact   2. Emile Durkheim
___ (c) manifest function   3. Karl Marx

<u>3. Match the research method with its appropriate form of data collection.</u>

___ (a) experiment   1. questionnaire
___ (b) survey   2. laboratory
___ (c) secondary analysis   3. existing statistics
___ (d) field research   4. case study

CHAPTER 2
CULTURE

Chapter Outline

Chapter Summary

Culture is the knowledge, language, values, customs, and material objects that are passed from person to person and from generation to generation. At the macrolevel, culture can be a stabilizing force or a source of conflict. At the microlevel, culture is essential for individual survival. Sociologists distinguish between **material culture**—the physical creations of society—and **nonmaterial culture**—abstract or intangible human. In Canada, diversity is reflected through race, ethnicity, age, sexual orientation, religion, occupation, and so forth. **Culture shock** refers to the anxiety people experience when they encounter cultures radically different from their own. **Ethnocentrism**—a belief based on the assumption that one's own culture is superior to others—is counterbalanced by **cultural relativism**—the belief that behaviours and customs of a society must be examined within the context of that culture.

Key Terms

counterculture (p. 62)
cultural imperialism (p. 70)
cultural lag (p. 58)
cultural relativism (p. 65)
cultural universals (p. 46)
culture (p. 42)
culture shock (p. 63)
diffusion (p. 57)
discovery (p. 56)
ethnocentrism (p. 64)
false consciousness (p. 67)
folkways (p. 55)
ideal culture (p. 55)
invention (p. 56)

language (p. 50)
laws (p. 56)
material culture (p. 46)
mores (p. 56)
nonmaterial culture (p. 46)
norms (p. 55)
real culture (p. 55)
sanctions (p. 55)
subculture (p. 61)
symbol (p. 48)
taboos (p. 56)
value contradictions (p. 54)
values (p. 53)

Review of Key Terms

_____ 1. Formal, standardized norms that have been enacted by legislatures.

_____ 2. Established rules of behaviour or standards of conduct.

_____ 3. Strongly held norms with moral and ethical connotations.

_____ 4. Rewards for appropriate behaviour or penalties for inappropriate acts.

_____ 5. Mores so strong that their violation is considered extremely offensive and even unmentionable.

_____ 6. Informal norms or everyday customs that may be violated without serious consequences.

_____ 7. The values and standards of behaviour that people in a society profess to hold.

_____ 8. Consists of the abstract or intangible human creations of society that influence people's behaviour.

_____ 9. Customs and practices that occur across all societies.

_____ 10. The knowledge, language, values, customs, and material objects that are passed from person to person and from one generation to the next.

_____ 11. Consists of the physical or tangible creations that members of a society make, use, and share.

_____ 12. A group that strongly rejects dominant societal values and norms and seeks alternative lifestyles.

_____ 13. A gap between the technical development of a society and its moral and legal institutions.

_____ 14. The belief that the behaviours and customs of a society must be viewed and analyzed within the context of its own culture.

_____ 15. The disorientation that people feel when they encounter cultures radically different from their own.

_____ 16. The assumption that one's own culture and way of life are superior to all others.

_____ 17. The extensive infusion of one nation's culture into other nations.

_____ 18. The transmission of cultural items or social practices from one group or society to another.

_____ 19. The process of learning about something previously unknown or unrecognized.

_____ 20. Holding beliefs that people think are in their best interests when those beliefs are actually damaging to their interests.

_____ 21. The process of reshaping existing cultural items into a new form.

_____ 22. A set of symbols that express ideas and enable people to think and communicate with one another.

_____ 23. Collective ideas about what is right or wrong, good or bad, and desirable or undesirable in a particular culture.

_____ 24. A group of people who share a distinctive set of cultural beliefs and behaviours that differ in some significant way from that of the larger society.

_____ 25. Values that conflict with one another or are mutually exclusive.

_____ 26. The values and standards of behaviour that people actually follow.

_____ 27. Anything that meaningfully represents somethings else.

Key People

Napoleon Chagnon (p. 63)   Bronislaw Malinowski (p. 66)
Marvin Harris (p. 65)   William F. Ogburn (p. 58)

Review of Key People

_____ 1. Experienced culture shock when he first encountered the Yanomamo, a tribe in South America.

_____ 2. Used cultural relativism to explain why cattle are not eaten in India despite widespread hunger and malnutrition.

_____ 3. Used the term cultural lag to refer the failure of nonmaterial culture to keep pace with material culture.

_____ 4. Suggested that culture helps people meet their biological, instrumental, and integral needs.

Learning Objectives

After reading Chapter 2 the student should be able to:

1. explain what culture is and describe how it can be both a stabilizing force and a source of conflict in societies (pp. 42-46).

2. define and distinguish between material and nonmaterial culture (p. 46).

3. be able to list and describe the four main components of culture (pp. 48-56).

4. describe the relationship between language and gender, and note how language is implicated in negative racial and ethnic stereotypes (pp. 50-51).

5. understand how language diversity affects Canadian culture (pp. 51-53).

6. list and briefly explain the core values in Canadian society (pp. 53-55).

7. contrast ideal and real culture and give examples of each (p. 55).

8. state the definition of norms and distinguish between folkways, mores, and laws (pp. 55-56).

9. distinguish between discovery, invention, and diffusion as means of cultural change. Explain why the rate of cultural change is uneven (pp. 56-58).

10. list the features of Canadian society that preclude the development of a readily identifiable Canadian culture (p. 61).

11. describe subcultures and countercultures, and give examples of each (pp. 61-63).

12. state the definitions for culture shock, ethnocentrism, and cultural relativism, and explain the relationship between these three concepts (pp. 63-66).

13. describe how the functionalist perspective views culture (pp. 66-67).

14. understand the assumptions of a conflict perspective on culture (p. 67).

15. explain how the interactionist view of culture differs from the structural functional and conflict perspectives (pp. 67-68).

16. outline the key cultural patterns for the 21st century (pp. 68-72).

Learning Objective Tests

Multiple Choice Questions

1. The relationship between language and gender is evident in the fact that:
   a. the English language ignores women through its use of masculine forms to refer to humans in general.
   b. when referring to occupations, pronouns tend to show the gender of the person we expect to hold that occupation.
   c. words are more likely to have positive connotations if they refer to men rather than women.
   d. all of the above examples show a relationship between language and gender.

2. The notions of equality and fairness in a democratic society represent:
   a. core Canadian values.
   b. positive sanctions.
   c. popular culture in Canada.
   d. ethnocentrism.

3. Thinking of yourself as a "good citizen" despite regularly driving over the speed limit demonstrates the distinction between:
   a. folkways and mores.
   b. ideal versus real culture.
   c. popular versus high culture.
   d. formal and informal norms.

4. Culture includes all of the following components EXCEPT:
   a. values.
   b. symbols.
   c. language.
   d. diversity.

5. Which of the following statements concerning culture is FALSE?
   a. Culture comprises ideas, behaviour, and material possessions.
   b. Culture can generate discord, conflict, and even violence.
   c. Culture exists independent of society.
   d. Culture can at times be a stabilizing force that provides a sense of continuity.

6. Cultural change, at both material and nonmaterial levels, is likely the result of:
   a. discovery.
   b. invention.
   c. diffusion.
   d. All of the above can contribute to cultural change.

7. Hutterites who live on farms in Western Canada can be considered a:
   a. subculture.
   b. counterculture.
   c. Xenocentrist group.
   d. population culture.

8. In 1969, the federal government passed the Official Languages Act:
   a. making French the official language of Quebec and English the official language for the remaining Canadian provinces.
   b. making French, English, and Ukrainian the official languages in Canada.
   c. making English the official language in Canada.
   d. making French and English official languages in Canada.

9. Cars, clothes, computers, and books are examples of:
   a. technology.
   b. nonmaterial culture.
   c. material culture.
   d. symbols.

10. If a Canadian teenager who was used to Rollerblades and computer games woke to find him or herself amongst the Yanomamo tribe of South America, he or she would immediately experience:
    a. cultural relativism.
    b. subcultures.
    c. culture shock.
    d. false consciousness.

11. As we enter the 21st century, we are likely to experience:
    a. a breakdown in the global culture that has existed for hundreds of years.
    b. an acceleration in the flow of information and expanded cultural diffusion.
    c. fewer single-parent families and less economic disparity.
    d. an end to cultural diversity and the emergence of a distinctly Canadian identity.

12. Which of the following is NOT one of the features of Canadian society that prevents it from developing a distinct Canadian identity?
    a. Canada is a vast territory with a disperse population.
    b. Canada has a high number of immigrants.
    c. There is an ongoing conflict between French- and English-speaking Canadians.
    d. The mass media are ineffective in transmitting cultural ideas and values.

13. Which perspective claims that values and norms help create and sustain the privileged position of the powerful in society while excluding others?
    a. functionalist
    b. conflict
    c. interactionist
    d. feminist

14. According to _____ theory, people continually negotiate their social realities.
    a. functionalist
    b. conflict
    c. interactionist
    d. feminist

15. Which perspective focuses on the needs of society and the fact that stability is essential for society's continued survival?
    a. functionalist
    b. conflict
    c. interactionist
    d. feminist

16. Not giving up your seat to an elderly or disabled person while riding on a city bus violates a:
    a. folkway.
    b. more.
    c. taboo.
    d. value.

True–False Statements

TF   1.   A central component of nonmaterial culture is beliefs (p. 46).

TF   2.   Recreational activities and social institutions are considered cultural universals because they exist in all societies (pp. 46-47).

TF   3.   The flower children of the 1960s and the drug enthusiasts of the 1970s are considered subcultures (pp. 62-63).

TF   4.   Culture could not exist without symbols because there would be no shared meanings among people (pp. 48-49).

TF   5.   Multiculturalism advocates tolerance of and encouragement for all cultural groups as vital to Canadian society (p. 61).

Fill-in-the-Blanks

1.   _____ provide ideals or beliefs about behaviour but do not state explicitly how we should behave (p. 53).

2.   Language, beliefs, values, rules of behaviour, family patterns, and political systems are examples of _____ _____ (p. 46).

3.   A _____ can stand for love such as a heart on a valentine (p. 48).

4.   _____ can create and reinforce our perceptions about race and ethnicity by transmitting preconceived ideas about the superiority of one category of people over another (p. 51).

Matching Items

1. Match each example with the corresponding type of norm.

___ (a) Standing up while the national anthem is playing.   1. taboo
___ (b) A sexual relationship between siblings.   2. folkway
___ (c) Committing first-degree murder.   3. law

2. Match each statement with the appropriate theoretical perspective.

___ (a) Culture meets biological and integrative needs.   1. functionalist
___ (b) Values are reinterpreted in every social situation.   2. conflict
___ (c) Values help maintain the positions of those in power.   3. interactionist

CHAPTER 3
SOCIALIZATION: FROM BIRTH TO OLD AGE

Chapter Outline

Chapter Summary

Socialization is the lifelong process through which individuals acquire a self-identity and the physical, mental, and social skills needed for survival. Social contact is essential in developing a self, or **self-concept.** Charles Horton Cooley developed the image of the **looking-glass self** to explain how people see themselves through the perceptions of others. George Herbert Mead linked the idea of self-concept to **role taking** and to learning the rules of social interaction. While Cooley's and Mead's theories are sociologically based, the theories of Sigmund Freud, Jean Piaget, Lawrence Kohlberg, and Carol Gilligan are based in psychology.

According to sociologists, **agents of socialization**—including families, schools, peer groups, and the media—teach us what we need to know in order to participate in society.

We learn knowledge and skills for future roles through **anticipatory socialization**. **Resocialization** involves learning new attitudes, values, and behaviours. Social class, gender, and race are determining factors in the lifelong socialization process. **Aging** includes the physical, psychological, and social processes associated with growing older. In Canada, the proportion of people aged 65 and older is increasing while the proportion of young people is decreasing. As we approach the 21st century, we must not only learn about the past but also acquire the knowledge and skills to think about the future in a practical manner.

Key Terms

ageism (p. 104)
agents of socialization (p. 91)
anticipatory socialization (p. 98)
catharsis theory (p. 95)
chronological age (p. 98)
ego (p. 87)
elder abuse (p. 107)
functional age (p. 98)
gender socialization (p. 98)
generalized other (p. 86)
hospice (p. 108)
id (p. 87)

looking-glass self (p. 84)
observational learning theory (p. 94)
peer group (p. 93)
resocialization (p. 96)
role-taking (p. 85)
self-concept (p. 82)
significant other (p. 85)
social genontology (p. 102)
socialization (p. 76)
superego (p. 87)
total institution (p. 97)

Review of Key Terms

_____ 1. Physical abuse, psychological abuse, financial exploitation, and medical abuse or neglect of people aged 65 or older.

_____ 2. Consists of the moral and ethical aspects of personality.

_____ 3. The rational, reality-oriented component of personality that imposes restrictions on the innate pleasure-seeking drives of the id.

_____ 4. The component of personality that includes all of the individual's basic biological drives and needs that demand immediate gratification.

_____ 5. Prejudice and discrimination against people on the basis of age.

_____ 6. The child's awareness of the demands and expectations of the society as a whole or of the child's subculture.

_____ 7. A group of people who are linked by common interests, equal social position, and (usually) similar age.

_____ 8. The lifelong process of social interaction through which individuals acquire a self-identity and the physical, mental, and social skills needed for survival in society.

_____ 9. The process by which a person mentally assumes the role of another person in order to understand the world from that person's point of view.

_____ 10. A person whose care, affection, and approval is especially desired and who is the most important in the development of the self.

_____ 11. The way in which a person's sense of self is derived from the perceptions of others.

_____ 12. The persons, groups, or institutions that teach us what we need to know in order to participate in society.

_____ 13. The aspect of socialization that contains specific messages and practices concerning the nature of being female or male in a specific group or society.

_____ 14. Suggests that violence in the media helps individuals relieve frustrations.

_____ 15. States that we observe the behaviour of another person and repeat the behaviour ourselves.

_____ 16. The process of learning a new and different set of attitudes, values, and behaviours from those in one's previous background and experience.

_____ 17. The totality of our beliefs and feelings about ourselves.

_____ 18. A place where people are isolated from the rest of society for a set period of time and come under the control of the officials who run the institution.

_____ 19. The process by which knowledge and skills are learned for future roles.

_____ 20. The study of the nonphysical aspects of aging.

_____ 21. A homelike facility that provides supportive care for patients with terminal illnesses.

_____ 22. A person's age based on date of birth.

_____ 23. Observable individual attributes such as physical appearance or mobility.

Key People

Charles Horton Cooley (p. 84)
Sigmund Freud (p. 87)
Carol Gilligan (p. 90)
Lawrence Kohlberg (p. 89)

George Herbert Mead (p. 85)
Wilbert Moore (p. 102)
Jean Piaget (p. 89)

Review of Key People

_____ 1. Believed that in each of four stages of cognitive development (from birth through adolescence), children's activities are governed by their perceptions of the world around them.

_____ 2. Criticized Kohlberg's research for its sole reliance on male subjects, claiming there was evidence of male–female differences with regard to morality.

_____ 3. Elaborated on Piaget's work, describing how morality develops.

_____ 4. Coined the term "looking-glass self."

_____ 5.   The founder of psychoanalytic theory.
_____ 6.   Described how the self develops, and divided the self into the "I" and the "me."
_____ 7.   Divided occupational socialization into four phases.

Learning Objectives

After reading Chapter 3 the student should be able to:

1. define socialization and explain why this process is essential for the individual and society (pp. 76-77).

2. explain why cases of isolated children are important to our understanding of the socialization process (pp. 79-82).

3. understand what is meant by the notions of "self-concept" and "self-identity" (pp. 82-83).

4. define Charles Horton Cooley's notion of the "looking-glass self" and explain how the looking-glass self develops (pp. 83-85).

5. explain the importance of "role-taking" and "significant others" to George Herbert Mead's theory of human development (p. 85).

6. be able to list and describe the three stages in the development of the self according to George Herbert Mead (pp. 85-86).

7. be able to list and describe the three components of personality central to Sigmund Freud's psychoanalytical perspective (pp. 87-89).

8. outline the stages of cognitive development as set forth by Jean Piaget (p. 89).

9. describe and distinguish between Lawrence Kohlberg's three stages of moral development (pp. 89-90).

10. be able to list the major agents of socialization (pp. 91-96)

11. describe how the family and the school system affect children's development (pp. 91-93).

12. describe the socializing roles of peer groups and the mass media (pp. 93-96).

13. explain what is meant by gender socialization (p. 98).

14. outline the stages of the life course and explain how each stage varies based on gender, ethnicity, class, and positive or negative treatment (p. 100-104).

15. discuss ageism and describe the negative stereotypes associated with older persons (p. 104-106).

Learning Objective Tests

Multiple Choice Questions

1. In which of Mead's stages of development does a child learn to use language and other symbols, taking on roles of others including a "doctor" or "superhero"?
   a. preparatory
   b. play
   c. game
   d. moral

2. The _____ would claim "I want that candy bar, no matter what!" according to Freud's theory of personality.
   a. id
   b. ego
   c. superego
   d. conscience

3. Which of the following is a major agent of socialization?
   a. the family
   b. mass media
   c. peer groups
   d. All of the above are agents of socialization.

4. Peer groups function as agents of socialization primarily by:
   a. contributing to our sense of "belonging" and self-worth.
   b. transmitting cultural and social values to us.
   c. providing an array of viewpoints on current issues.
   d. introducing us to a wide variety of people.

5. Which of the following statements about socialization is FALSE?
   a. Socialization is essential for human development.
   b. Socialization is a lifelong process.
   c. The content of socialization is basically the same from one society to another.
   d. The socialization process is more effective when people conform to the norms of society.

6.   Our perception of what kind of person we are is known as our:
   a.   ego.
   b.   id.
   c.   self-concept.
   d.   self-identity.

7.   All of the following form the basis of Kohlberg's stages of moral development
     EXCEPT the:
   a.   preconventional level.
   b.   formal level.
   c.   conventional level.
   d.   postconventional level.

8.   The cases of "Anna" and "Genie" illustrate that:
   a.   successful socialization results in the absence of human contact.
   b.   the effects of social isolation on humans cannot be determined with any
        accuracy.
   c.   the behaviour of humans is totally dissimilar to that of nonhuman primates.
   d.   socialization is unsuccessful in the absence of early social interaction.

9.   The looking-glass self is:
   a.   who we actually are.
   b.   what people actually think of us.
   c.   based on our perception of how other people think of us.
   d.   our perception about what kind of person we are.

10.   _____ emphasized the role of significant others in the development of the self.
   a.   Charles Horton Cooley
   b.   George Herbert Mead
   c.   Sigmund Freud
   d.   Jean Piaget

11.   Anticipatory socialization practices are most closely associated with which stage in
      the life course?
   a.   infancy and childhood
   b.   adolescence
   c.   middle adulthood
   d.   older adulthood

12.   In which of Piaget's developmental stages can children draw conclusions about the
      likely physical consequences of an action without always having to try it out?
   a.   sensorimotor
   b.   preoperational
   c.   concrete operational
   d.   formal operational

13. Responding differently to male and female infants by playing more roughly with boys and talking more lovingly to girls illustrates:
    a. social devaluation.
    b. anticipatory socialization.
    c. gender socialization.
    d. total institution.

14. According to functionalists, schools are responsible for:
    a. teaching students to be productive members of society.
    b. transmitting culture.
    c. social control and personal development.
    d. all of the above.

15. The media contributes to ageism by:
    a. portraying older persons as doddering, feebleminded, wrinkled, and laughable.
    b. portraying older persons as unattractive and incompetent.
    c. conveying the subtle message that older women are especially unimportant.
    d. all of the above.

True–False Statements

TF   1. The media contributes to ageism in its portrayal of older persons as feebleminded individuals (p. 104).

TF   2. When a person is well adjusted, the ego successfully manages the opposing forces of the id and the superego (p. 87).

TF   3. During Mead's play stage, children understand not only their own social position but also the positions of others around them (p. 85).

TF   4. Child abuse includes physical abuse, sexual abuse, physical neglect, and emotional mistreatment (p. 82).

TF   5. Socialization ends in older adulthood (p. 98).

TF   6. Cooley asserted that we base our perception of who we are on how we think other people see us and on whether this seems good or bad to us (p. 84).

TF   7. Families are the primary source of emotional support (p. 91).

TF   8. Involuntary resocialization occurs against a person's wishes and generally takes place within a total institution (p. 97).

TF   9. The poverty rate for elderly women is double that of elderly men (p. 106).

TF   10.   Young women will be less able to deal with the financial pressures of old age as a result of structural changes in Canadian society (p. 107).

Fill-in-the-Blanks

1.   The family, school, mass media, and peer groups are _____ of _____ (p. 91).

2.   The _____ - _____ _____ is based on our perception of how other people think of us (p. 84).

3.   During the _____ _____, up to about age 3, interactions lack meaning, and children largely imitate the people around them (p. 85).

4.   _____ is essential for an individual's survival and for human development (p. 76).

5.   _____ socialization is one of the most important types of adult socialization (p. 102).

6.   In early childhood, _____ _____ are often composed of classmates in daycare, preschool, and elementary school (p. 93).

7.   The _____ _____ is comprised of large-scale organizations that use print or electronic means to communicate with large numbers of people (p. 94).

8.   The new-born baby's personality is all _____, and from birth the child finds that urges for self-gratification will not be satisfied immediately (p. 87).

9.   Mead extended Cooley's insights by linking the idea of self-concept to _____ - _____ (the process by which a person mentally assumes the role of another) (p. 85).

10.   Our _____ _____ is our perception about what kind of person we are (p. 83).

Matching Items

1. Match the concept with the appropriate theorist.

___ (a) looking-glass self   1. Sigmund Freud
___ (b) superego   2. Charles Cooley
___ (c) generalized other   3. Lawrence Kohlberg
___ (d) conventional level   4. Jean Piaget
___ (e) formal operational stage   5. George Herbert Mead

CHAPTER 4
SOCIAL STRUCTURE, SOCIAL INTERACTION, AND COLLECTIVE BEHAVIOUR

Chapter Outline

Chapter Summary

Social structure and interaction are critical components of everyday life. **Social interaction**—the process by which people act toward or respond to other people—is the foundation of meaningful relationships. At the macrolevel, **social structure** is the stable pattern of social relationships that exists within a particular group or society. This structure includes social institutions, groups, statuses, roles, and norms. Social interaction is guided by shared meanings of how we behave while our perception of those meanings is influenced by race, ethnicity, gender, and social class. The **social construction of reality** refers to the process by which our perception of reality is shaped by the subjective meaning we give to an experience. **Dramaturgical analysis** is the study of social interaction that compares everyday life to a theatrical presentation. **Presentation of self** refers to efforts to present our own self to others in ways that are most favourable to our own interests or image. Social interaction is also marked by **nonverbal**

communication, which is the transfer of information between people without the use of speech. **Social change** is the alteration, modification, or transformation of public policy, culture, or social institutions over time. Such change usually is brought about by **collective behaviour**—voluntary, often spontaneous activity that is engaged in by a large number of people and typically violates dominant group norms and values. Five categories of crowds have been identified: (1) casual crowds are relatively large gatherings of people who happen to be in the same place at the same time; (2) conventional crowds comprise people who specifically come together for a scheduled event and thus share a common focus; (3) expressive crowds provide opportunities for the expression of some strong emotion; (4) acting crowds are collectivities so intensely focused on a specific purpose or object that they may erupt into violent or destructive behaviour; and (5) protest crowds are gatherings of people who engage in activities intended to achieve specific political goals. Explanations of crowd behaviour include contagion theory, convergence theory, and emergent norm theory. Examples of **mass behaviour**—collective behaviour that takes place when people respond to the same event in much the same way—include rumours, gossip, fads, fashions, and public opinion. The major types of **social movements**—organized groups that act consciously to promote or resist change through collective action—are reform movements, revolutionary movements, religious movements, alternative movements, and resistance movements.

Key Terms

achieved status (p. 119)

ascribed status (p. 118)

civil disobedience (p. 139)

collective behaviour (p. 135)

crowd (p. 136)

dramaturgical analysis (p. 129)

fad (p. 141)

fashion (p. 142)

formal organization (p. 124)

gossip (p. 141)

mass (p. 136)

mass behaviour (p. 141)

master status (p. 119)

mob (p. 120)

nonverbal communication (p. 132)

panic (p. 138)

personal space (p. 134)

presentation of self (p. 129)

primary group (p. 122)

propaganda (p. 142)

public opinion (p. 142)

riot (p. 138)

role (p. 120)

role conflict (p. 121)

role exit (p. 122)

role expectation (p. 120)

role performance (p. 120)

role strain (p. 121)

rumours (p. 141)

secondary group (p. 122)

self-fulfilling prophecy (p. 128)

social construction of reality (p. 128)

social group (p. 122)

social institution (p. 124)

social interaction (p. 114)

social marginality (p. 116)

social movement (p. 143)

social network (p. 123)

social structure (p. 114)

status (p. 118)

status set (p. 118)

status symbol (p. 120)

stigma (p. 116)

terrorism (p. 144)

Review of Key Terms

_____ 1. Violent crowd behaviour that is fueled by deep-seated emotions but not directed at one specific target.

_____ 2. Relatively spontaneous, unstructured activity that typically violates established social norms.

_____ 3. Is the immediate area surrounding a person that the person claims is private.

_____ 4. Is a set of behavioural expectations associated with a given status.

_____ 5. Occurs when people disengage from social roles that have been central to their self-identity.

_____ 6. A false belief or prediction that produces behaviour that makes the originally false belief come true.

_____ 7. A number of people who share an interest in a specific idea or issue but who are not in one another's immediate vicinity.

_____ 8. A highly emotional crowd whose members engage in, or are ready to engage in, violence against a specific target, a person, a category of people, or physical property.

_____ 9. A number of people who share an interest in a specific idea or issue but are not in one another's immediate vicinity.

_____ 10. Is a group's or society's definition of the way a specific role _ought_ to be played.

_____ 11. Is how a person _actually_ plays a role in society.

_____ 12. Are material signs that inform others of a person's specific status.

_____ 13. The calculated unlawful use of physical force or threats of violence against persons or property in order to intimidate or coerce a government, organization, or individual for the purpose of gaining some political, religious, economic, or social objective.

_____ 14. A relatively large number of people who are in one another's immediate vicinity.

_____ 15. Are unsubstantiated reports on an issue or subject.

_____ 16. A temporary but widely copied activity enthusiastically followed by large numbers of people.

_____ 17. Collective behaviour that takes place when people respond to the same event in much the same way.

_____ 18. Consists of the political attitudes and beliefs communicated by ordinary citizens to decision makers.

_____ 19. Information provided by individuals or groups that have a vested rest in furthering their own cause or damaging an opposing one.

_____ 20. An organized group that acts consciously to promote or resist change through collective action.

_____ 21. A form of crowd behaviour that occurs when a large number of people react to a real or perceived threat with strong emotions and self-destructive behaviour.

_____ 22. Rumours about the personal lives of individuals.

_____ 23. Is a series of social relationships that link an individual to others.

_____ 24. A set of organized beliefs and rules that establish how a society will attempt to meets its basic social needs.

_____ 25. A highly structured group formed for the purpose of completing certain tasks or achieving specific goals.

_____ 26. Consists of two or more people who interact frequently and share a common identity and a feeling of interdependence.

_____ 27. Is the state of being part insider and part outsider in the social structure.

_____ 28. The process by which our perception of reality is shaped largely by the subjective meaning that we give to an experience.

_____ 29. Occurs when incompatible role demands are placed on a person by two or more statuses held at the same time.

_____ 30. Occurs when incompatible demands are built into a single status that a person occupies.

_____ 31. The transfer of information between persons without the use of speech.

_____ 32. The study of social interaction that compares everyday life to a theatrical presentation.

_____ 33. People's efforts to present themselves to others in ways that are most favourable to their own interests or image.

_____ 34. The stable pattern of social relationships that exist within a particular group or society.

_____ 35. The process by which people act toward or respond to other people.

_____ 36. A social position conferred at birth or received involuntarily later in life.

_____ 37. A social position a person assumes voluntarily as a result of personal choice, merit, or direct effort.

_____ 38. The most important status that a person occupies and that dominates all others.

_____ 39. A socially defined position in a group or society characterized by certain expectations, rights, and duties.

_____ 40. Includes all the statuses that a person occupies at a given time.

_____ 41. Any physical or social attribute that devalues a person's social identity.

_____ 42. A larger, more specialized group in which members engage in more impersonal, goal-oriented relationships for a limited period of time.

_____ 43. A small, less specialized group in which members engage in face-to-face, emotion-based interactions over an extended period of time.

_____ 44. The study of social interaction that compares everyday life to a theatrical presentation.

_____ 45. Nonviolent action that seeks to change a policy or law by refusing to comply with it.

Key People

Daniel and Cheryl Albas (p. 129)   Clark McPhail and Ronald T. Wohlstein (p. 139)
Erving Goffman (p. 123)   Georg Simmel (p. 142)
Edward Hall (p. 134)   Ralph H. Turner and
Helen Rose Fuchs Ebaugh (p. 122)   Lewis M. Killian (p. 136)
Gustave Le Bon (p. 140)   Jacqueline Wiseman (p. 129)
John Lofland (p. 142)

Review of Key People

_____ 1. Argued that people are more likely to engage in antisocial behaviour in a crowd because they are anonymous and feel invulnerable.

_____ 2. Suggested a "trickle-down" theory of fashion.

_____ 3. Analyzed how students present themselves to one another after receiving exam grades.

_____ 4. Found that homeless people living on skid row evaluated their situation more positively than the social workers who dealt with them.

_____ 5. Analyzed the physical distance between people speaking to one another and found that the amount of personal space people prefer varies from one culture to another.

_____ 6. Suggested that day-to-day interactions have much in common with being on stage or in a dramatic production.

_____ 7. Suggested that fear, hostility, and joy are three fundamental emotions found in collective behaviour.

_____ 8. Added protest crowds to the four types identified by Blumer.

_____ 9. Developed emergent norm theory.

_____ 10. Studied role exit by interviewing ex-convicts, ex-nuns, and divorced individuals.

Learning Objectives

After reading Chapter 4, the student should be able to:

1. state the definition of social interaction and social structure and explain why these concepts are important for individuals and society (pp. 114-117).

2. explain what is meant by "social marginality" and "stigma," and describe the relationship between these terms (pp. 116-117).

3. state the definition of status and distinguish between ascribed and achieved statuses (pp. 118-119).

4. explain what is meant by "master status" and provide an example of one (pp. 119-120).

5. define "role" and note the difference between a role expectation and a role performance (p. 120).

6. understand the difference between role conflict and role strain, and be able to provide an example of each (p. 121).

7. describe the process of role exiting (p. 122).

8. explain the difference in primary and secondary groups (p. 122).

9. define formal organization (p. 124)

10. state the definition for social institution and name the major institutions found in contemporary society (p. 124).

11. evaluate functionalist and conflict perspectives on the nature and purpose of social institutions (pp. 124-125).

12. explain what interactionists mean by the social construction of reality (p. 128).

13. describe Goffman's dramaturgical analysis and explain what he meant by presentation of self (p. 129)).

14. explain Goffman's notion of "face-saving behaviour" and provide an example that illustrates how face-saving behaviour operates in everyday life (pp. 131-132).

15. define nonverbal communication and explain why it is important in social interactions (pp. 132-135).

16. state the definition for personal space and describe the "distance zones" identified by Hall (p. 134).

17. define collective behaviour and describe the conditions necessary for such behaviour to occur (pp. 135-136).

18. list and describe the three questions that help us understand the dynamics of collective behaviour (p. 136).

19. distinguish between crowds and masses (pp. 136-137).

20. define and distinguish between casual, conventional, expressive, acting, and protest crowds (pp. 137-139).

21. discuss the key assumptions of contagion theory (p. 140).

22. discuss the key assumptions of convergence theory (p. 140).

23. discuss the key assumptions of emergent norm theory (pp. 140-141).

24. define mass behaviour and distinguish between the most frequent types (pp. 141–142).

25. differentiate among the five major types of social movements based on their goals and the degree of change they seek to produce (pp. 143-146).

Learning Objective Tests

Multiple Choice Questions

1. Being wealthy influences many other aspects of life, including health, leisure, and education. Being wealthy is:
   a. a status set.
   b. a status role.
   c. social stigma.
   d. master status.

2. Which of the following examples best illustrates stigmatization?
   a. a convicted criminal who must wear a prison uniform
   b. a steel worker who receives a promotion to foreman
   c. a woman who earns a master's degree in psychology
   d. a soldier who wears a medal of honour

3. All of the following are examples of formal organizations EXCEPT:
   a. colleges.
   b. families.
   c. corporations.
   d. government.

4. Ex-convicts, ex-nuns, divorcees, and retirees have all undergone:
   a. master status.
   b. role strain.
   c. dramaturgical analyses.
   d. role exit.

5. Which perspective claims that social institutions maintain the privileges of the wealthy and powerful while contributing to the powerlessness of others?
   a. functional
   b. conflict
   c. interactionist
   d. dramaturgical

6. A peace officer is likely to view the scene of a crime much differently than a criminal or a victim. Interactionists describe how people define the same situation in different ways as:
   a. the social construction of reality.
   b. face-saving behaviour.
   c. social structure.
   d. self-fulfilling prophecy.

7. John is a father, husband, college graduate, and convicted criminal. This example describes John's:
   a. status symbols.
   b. ascribed statuses.
   c. achieved statuses.
   d. social structure.

8. _____ is essential for the survival of society and for the well-being of individuals because it provides a web of familial support and social relationships that connect each of us to the larger society.
   a. social interaction
   b. social structure
   c. social status
   d. social space

9. A student who shows up late for class, speaks out of turn, and stands facing the class instead of sitting in her seat has violated:
   a. a status set.
   b. a social network.
   c. role expectations.
   d. status roles.

10. Susan is torn between going to her mother's for supper, spending time with her nephew, or working late at the office. Susan is experiencing:
    a. role conflict.
    b. role strain.
    c. role ambiguity.
    d. role exit.

11. Close friends and family members form the basis of:
    a. Gemenschaft.
    b. Gesellschaft.
    c. primary groups.
    d. secondary groups.

12. All of the following are major social institutions EXCEPT:
    a. the family.
    b. religion.
    c. the government.
    d. All of the above are major social institutions.

13. Which of Hall's (1966) distance zones extends beyond four metres?
    a. intimate distance
    b. personal distance
    c. social distance
    d. public distance

14. Presentation of self refers to people's efforts to:
    a. rescue their performance after experiencing loss of face.
    b. compare everyday life to a theatrical presentation.
    c. understand the situations in which they find themselves.
    d. present themselves to others in ways most favourable to their own interests.

15. Nonverbal communication includes:
    a. facial expressions.
    b. head movements.
    c. body movements.
    d. all of the above.

16. After receiving a low grade on an exam, Mark claimed that he was ill on the day of the test and that some of the test questions were unfair. This example demonstrates:
    a. face-saving behaviour.
    b. role conflict.
    c. role strain.
    d. social marginality.

17. All of the following are major contributors to collective behaviour EXCEPT:
    a. structural factors, including larger causes.
    b. timing.
    c. clearly established norms.
    d. a breakdown in social control.

18. Which of the following is a key question that helps us understand collective behaviour?
    a. How do people come to transcend or bypass established institutional patterns and structures?
    b. How do people's actions compare with their attitudes?
    c. Why do people act collectively rather than alone?
    d. All of the above questions help us understand collective behaviour.

19. Religious services, graduation ceremonies, concerts, and college classes are examples of:
    a. casual crowds.
    b. conventional crowds.
    c. expressive crowds.
    d. active crowds.

20. A number of people who share an interest in a specific issue but are not in one another's immediate vicinity make up a:
    a. crowd.
    b. mass.
    c. aggregate.
    d. none of the above.

21. Firebombings and hate crimes that are directed against a specific target by a highly emotional crowd are examples of:
    a. mob behaviour.
    b. riots.
    c. panic.
    d. civil disobedience.

22. Which theory assumes that some people have a predisposition to participate in collectivities with like-minded persons with whom they can express themselves?
    a. contagion
    b. convergence
    c. emergent norm
    d. mass hysteria

23. Turner and Killian's emergent norm theory is used to explain:
    a. the shared emotions, goals, and beliefs many people bring to crowd behaviour.
    b. how a crowd takes on a life of its own as a result of anonymity.
    c. how moods, attitudes, and behaviour are communicated rapidly and why they are accepted by others.
    d. how individuals in a given collectivity develop an understanding of what is going on, and how they construe these activities.

24. A movement that seeks to remake the entire system by replacing existing institutions with new ones is a:
    a. reform movement.
    b. revolutionary movement.
    c. religious movement.
    d. alternative movement.

25. Stories that concern the personal lives of individuals that are often reported in tabloids such as the *National Enquirer* or *People* magazine represent:
    a. rumours.
    b. gossip.
    c. public opinion.
    d. urban legends.

True–False Statements

TF   1. Social interaction is the foundation for all relationships and groups in society (p. 114).

TF   2. Social marginality can result in stigmatization (p. 116).

TF   3. Ethnicity, age, and gender are examples of achieved statuses (p. 119).

TF   4. We occupy a role, we play a status (p. 120).

TF   5. Statuses exist independently of the specific people occupying them (p. 118).

TF   6. When people are proud of a particular social status they occupy, they often choose visible means to let others know about their position (p. 120).

TF   7. Role ambiguity occurs when the expectations associated with a role are unclear (p. 120).

TF   8. A riot is a form of crowd behaviour that occurs when a large number of people react to a real or perceived threat with strong emotions and self-destructive behaviour (p. 138).

TF   9. Riots are often triggered by fear, anger, and hostility (p. 138).

TF   10. Protest crowds engage in activities intended to achieve specific political goals (p. 139).

TF   11. Gustave Le Bon argued that people are more likely to engage in antisocial behaviour in a crowd because they are anonymous and feel invulnerable (p. 140).

TF   12.   According to contagion theory, people with similar attributes find a collectivity of like-minded persons with whom they can express their underlying personal tendencies (p. 140).

TF   13.   Emergent norms occur when people define a new situation as highly unusual or see a long-standing situation in a new light (p. 141).

TF   14.   Collective behaviour is longer lasting and more organized than social movements (p. 143).

TF   15.   Social movements provide people who otherwise would not have the resources to enter the game of politics a chance to do so (p. 143).

TF   16.   Members of reform movements usually work within the existing system to attempt to change existing public policy so that it more adequately reflects their own values systems (p. 143).

TF   17.   Resistance movements seek to prevent change or to undo change that already has occurred (p. 144).

Fill-in-the-Blanks

1.   We _____ a status, we _____ a role (p. 120).

2.   In addition to providing a map for our encounters with others, _____ _____ may limit our options and place us in arbitrary categories not of our own choosing (p. 116).

3.   A _____ _____ is comprised of all the statuses that a person occupies at a given time (p. 118).

4.   A _____ _____ dominates all of the individual's other statuses and is the overriding ingredient in determining a person's general social position (p. 119).

5.   Driving a Rolls-Royce is a _____ _____ that informs others of the driver's wealth (p. 120).

6.   _____ _____ occurs when role expectations are unclear (p. 120).

7.   A _____ _____ is a small, less specialized group in which members engage in face-to-face, emotion-based interactions over an extended period of time (p. 122).

8.   Many of us spend most of our time in _____ _____, such as universities, corporations, or the government (p. 122).

9. A group is composed of specific, identifiable people; an _____ is a standardized way of doing something (p. 124).

10. _____ _____ are made up of people who specifically come together for a scheduled event and thus share a common focus (p. 137).

11. Mobs, riots, and panics are examples of _____ crowds, collectivities so intensely focused on a specific purpose or object that they may erupt into violent or destructive behaviour (p. 137).

12. Protest crowds sometimes take the form of _____ _____, in which nonviolent action is taken in an attempt to change a policy or law by refusing to comply with it (p. 139).

13. Unlike contagion and convergence theories, _____ _____ _____ emphasizes the importance of social norms in shaping crowd behaviour (p. 140).

14. Whereas rumours deal with an issue or a subject, _____ refers to rumours about the personal lives of individuals (p. 141).

15. Movements seeking to bring about a total change in society are referred to as _____ (p. 143).

16. Movements that seek limited change in some aspect of people's behaviour such as abstinence from drinking alcohol are referred to as _____ (p. 144).

Matching Items

1. Match the example with the appropriate type of crowd.

___ (a) scheduled events   1. casual
___ (b) shoppers in a mall   2. conventional
___ (c) worships or mourners   3. expressive
___ (d) mobs and riots   4. acting
___ (e) civil disobedience   5. protest

2. Match the concept with the appropriate theory of collective behaviour.

___ (a) common attributes   1. contagion theory
___ (b) deindividuation   2. convergence theory
___ (c) definition of the situation   3. emergent norm theory

CHAPTER 5
GROUPS AND ORGANIZATIONS

Chapter Outline

Chapter Summary

Groups are a key element of our social structure and much of our social interaction takes place within them. A **social group** is a collection of two or more people who interact frequently, share a sense of belonging, and have a feeling of interdependence. Social groups may be either **primary groups**—small, personal groups in which members engage in emotion-based interactions over an extended period—or **secondary groups**—larger, more specialized groups in which members have less personal and more formal, goal-oriented relationships. All groups set boundaries to indicate who does and who does not belong: an **ingroup** is a group to which we belong and with which we identify; an **outgroup** is a group we do not belong to or perhaps feel hostile toward. The size of a group is one of its most important features. The smallest groups are **dyads**—groups composed of two members—and **triads**—groups of three. In order to maintain ties with a group, many members are willing to conform to norms established and reinforced by group members. Three types of **formal organizations**—highly structured secondary groups formed to achieve specific goals in an efficient manner—are normative, coercive, and utilitarian organizations. A **bureaucracy** is a formal organization characterized by hierarchical authority, division of labour, explicit procedures, and impersonality in personnel concerns. As we approach the 21st century, all of us benefit from organizations that operate humanely and that include opportunities for all, regardless of race, gender, or class.

Key Terms

aggregate (p. 153)
authoritarian leaders (p. 160)
bureaucracy (p. 167)
bureaucratic personality (p. 171)
category (p. 154)
conformity (p. 159)
democratic leaders (p. 160)
dyad (p. 159)
expressive leaders (p. 160)
goal displacement (p. 170)

informal structure (p. 169)
ingroup (p. 157)
instrumental leadership (p. 160)
laissez-faire leaders (p. 160)
outgroup (p. 157)
rationality (p. 168)
reference group (p. 158)
small group (p. 159)
triad (p. 160)

Review of Key Terms

_____ 1. A number of people who may never have met one another but share a similar characteristic (such as education level).

_____ 2. A group to which a person does not belong and toward which the person may feel a sense of competitiveness or hostility.

_____ 3. A group to which a person belongs and with which the person feels a sense of identity.

_____ 4. A collection of people who happen to be in the same place at the same time but share little else in common.

_____ 5. A collectivity small enough for all members to be acquainted with one another and to interact simultaneously.

_____ 6. The process of maintaining or changing behaviour to comply with the norms established by a society, subculture, or other group.

_____ 7. Make all major group decisions and assign tasks to members.

_____ 8. Describes workers who are more concerned with following correct procedures than they are with getting the job done correctly.

_____ 9. An organizational model characterized by a hierarchy of authority, a clear division of labour, explicit rules and procedures, and impersonality.

_____ 10. A group that strongly influences a person's behaviour and social attitudes, regardless of whether that individual is an actual member.

_____ 11. Provide emotional support to their group members.

_____ 12. Encourage group discussion and decision making through consensus building.

_____ 13. A group composed of only two members.

_____ 14. The process by which traditional methods of social organization, characterized by informality and spontaneity, gradually are replaced by efficiently administered formal rules and procedures.

_____ 15. Occurs when rules become an end in themselves rather than a means to an end, and organizational survival becomes more important than achievement of goals.

_____ 16. A group composed of exactly three members.

_____ 17. Are only minimally involved in decision making and encourage group members to make their own decisions.

_____ 18. Composed of those aspects of participants' day-to-day activities and interactions that ignore, bypass, or do not correspond with the official rules and procedures of the bureaucracy.

_____ 19. Leadership that is goal- or task-oriented.

Key People

Solomon Asch (p. 161)
Charles H. Cooley (p. 157)
Amitai Etzioni (p. 165)
Stanley Milgram (p.162)

Georg Simmel (p. 159)
William Graham Sumner (p. 157)
Max Weber (p. 168)

Review of Key People

_____ 1. Classified formal organizations into normative, coercive, or utilitarian.

_____ 2. Studied group pressure to conform using estimations of line length.

_____ 3. Used the term primary group to describe small, less specialized groups in which members engage in face-to-face emotion-based interactions.

_____ 4. Was interested in the historical trend toward bureaucratization that accelerated during the Industrial Revolution and used an ideal-type to represent this phenomenon.

_____ 5. Coined the terms *ingroup* and *outgroup.*

_____ 6. Studied obedience to authority through willingness to administer electric shocks.

_____ 7. Suggested that small groups (e.g., dyads) have distinctive interaction patterns that do not exist in larger groups.

Learning Objectives

After reading Chapter 5, the student should be able to:

1. distinguish between aggregates and categories from a sociological perspective (pp. 153-154).

2. distinguish between primary and secondary groups and explain how people's relationships differ in each (p. 157).

3. state definitions for ingroup, outgroup, and reference group, and describe the significance of these concepts in everyday life (pp. 157-159).

4. describe dyads and triads and explain how interaction patterns change as the size of a group increases (pp. 159-160).

5. be able to distinguish between the two functions of leadership (p. 160).

6. be able to list and distinguish among the three major styles of group leadership (pp. 160-161).

7. briefly describe the procedures and findings of Solomon Asch and Stanley Milgram's research, noting how the results contribute to our understanding of conformity (pp. 161-163).

8. explain how group conformity is implicated in sexual harassment (pp. 163-164).

9. compare normative, coercive, and utilitarian organizations, and describe the nature of membership in each (pp. 165-167).

10. be able to define bureaucracy and summarize Max Weber's perspective on rationality (pp. 167-168).

11. be able to list and describe the characteristics of Weber's ideal-type bureaucracy (p. 168).

12. describe the informal structure in bureaucracies and list its positive and negative aspects (pp. 169-170).

13. discuss how inefficiency and rigidity leads to problems for bureaucratic administrators and workers (pp. 170-172).

14. highlight the major shortcomings of bureaucracies in resisting change and perpetuating ethnic, class, and gender inequalities (pp. 172-173).

15. compare and contrast North American and Japanese models of organization (pp. 174-176).

Learning Objective Tests

Multiple Choice Questions

1. Suppose you play for the Edmonton Oilers hockey team. In this case, the Calgary Flames team would be considered your:
    a. primary group.
    b. ingroup.
    c. outgroup.
    d. aggregate.

2. A large, impersonal, goal-oriented group is a(n):
    a. dyad.
    b. ingroup.
    c. primary group.
    d. secondary group.

3. We voluntarily join this kind of organization in order to obtain material rewards:
    a. normative organizations
    b. coercive organizations
    c. utilitarian organizations
    d. bureaucracies

4. John Pryors' (1992) experiments on the social dynamics of harassment showed that:
    a. When given the opportunity to do so, only 10 percent of the participants sexually harassed a victim.
    b. Males were more likely to be victims of sexual harassment than females.
    c. Women and men were equally likely to be perpetrators of sexual harassment.
    d. Men who believed that sexual harassment was condoned, harassed a female victim in 90 percent of the cases.

5. Shoppers in a department store and passengers on a bus are examples of a(n):
    a. category.
    b. aggregate.
    c. primary group.
    d. ingroup.

6. What type of leadership provides emotional support for members?
    a. instrumental
    b. expressional
    c. democratic
    d. authoritarian

7. Asch's research using line length showed that group pressure is influenced by:
   a. size of the group.
   b. degree of social cohesion.
   c. a and b.
   d. none of the above.

8. In a bureaucracy, information often spreads faster through the "grapevine" than through official channels. This illustrates:
   a. hierarchy of authority.
   b. inefficiency and rigidity.
   c. informal structures in bureaucracies.
   d. impersonality in bureaucracies.

9. Which leadership style would be most effective in a situation where members work independently with little direction to achieve goals?
   a. authoritarian
   b. democratic
   c. laissez-faire
   d. expressive

10. Married couples form the basis of a(n):
    a. category.
    b. dyad.
    c. secondary group.
    d. outgroup.

11. The process by which traditional methods are replaced by efficiently administered formal rules is:
    a. bureaucracy.
    b. rationality.
    c. utilitarianism.
    d. coercion.

12. Which of the following is NOT one of Weber's ideal characteristics of bureaucracy?
    a. hierarchy of authority.
    b. specialization in the division of labour.
    c. standard rules and regulations.
    d. employment based on favouritism or family connection.

13. A prime example of rigidity in bureaucracy is:
    a. lifetime employment.
    b. quality circles.
    c. information structure.
    d. goal displacement.

14. Which of the following is a major shortcoming of bureaucracies?
    a. inefficiency and rigidity
    b. resistance to change
    c. perpetuation of ethnic, class, and gender inequalities
    d. All of the above are major shortcomings of bureaucracy

15. The key difference between Japanese and North American corporations is:
    a. Japanese employees often remain with the same company for their entire career.
    b. Cultural traditions in Japan focus on the importance of individuals over the group.
    c. Women fare better than men in Japanese organizations.
    d. Japan has a history of labour-management disputes.

True–False Statements

TF 1. Sexual harassment is not a criminal offence in Canada (p. 156).

TF 2. An outgroup is a group to which a person belongs and with which that person feels a sense of identity (p. 157).

TF 3. Democratic leaders encourage group members to make decisions on their own (pp. 160-161).

TF 4. Instrumental leadership is most appropriate when the group's purpose is to complete a task or reach a particular goal (p. 160).

TF 5. Over the past century, the number of formal organizations has increased dramatically in Canada (p. 164).

Fill-in-the-Blanks

1. People in _____ share a common purpose but generally do not interact with one another (pp. 153-154).

2. William Graham Sumner coined the terms _____ and _____ to describe people's feelings toward members of their own and other groups (p. 157).

3. A _____ is a group that consists of only two members (p. 159).

4. _____ leaders may be criticized for being dictatorial and for fostering ingroup hostility (p. 160).

5. We voluntarily join _____ organizations when they can provide us with the material rewards we seek (p. 167).

Matching Items

1. Match the leadership style with the appropriate group characteristic:

___ (a) authoritarian

1. decision making results from group discussion

___ (b) democratic

2. members carry out tasks under direct orders

___ (c) laissez-faire

3. members make decisions on their own

CHAPTER 6
DEVIANCE AND CRIME

Chapter Outline

Chapter Summary

All societies have norms to reinforce and help teach acceptable behavior. They also have mechanisms of **social control**—practices developed by social groups to encourage conformity and to discourage **deviance**—any behaviour, belief, or condition that violates cultural norms. **Crime** is a form of deviant behaviour that violates criminal law and is punishable by fines, jail terms, and other sanctions. Functionalists use **strain theory,** and **social bonding theory** to argue that socialization into the value of material success without the corresponding legitimate means to achieve that goal accounts for a large portion of crime. Interactionists use **differential association theory** and **labelling theory** to explain how a person's behaviour is influenced by others. Conflict theorists suggest that people with economic and political power define as criminal any behaviour that threatens their own interests. Feminist approaches focus on the intertwining of gender, class, race, ethnicity, and deviance. While the law classifies crime into summary convictions and indictable offences based on its seriousness, sociologists categorize crimes according to how they are committed and how society views them. Three general categories of crime include: **occupational, organized** and **street crimes.** Studies show that many more crimes are committed than are reported in official statistics. Gender, age, class, and race are key factors in official crime statistics. The criminal justice system includes the police, courts, and prisons—agencies that have considerable discretion in dealing with deviance. As we move into the 21st century, we need new approaches for dealing with crime and delinquency. We also need to insure an equal justice system for all, regardless of race, class, sex, or age.

Key Terms

corporate crime (p. 197)
crime (p. 186)
deviance (p. 183)
differential association theory (p. 190)
illegitimate opportunity structures (p. 187)
juvenile delinquency (p. 186)
labelling theory (p. 191)
occupational crime (p. 197)

organized crime (p. 198)
primary deviance (p. 192)
punishment (p. 207)
secondary deviance (p. 192)
social bond theory (p. 189)
social control (p. 183)
strain theory (p. 187)
street crime (p. 194)

Review of Key Terms

_____ 1. Any action designed to deprive a person of things of value because of some offence the person is thought to have committed.

_____ 2. A violation of law by young people under the age of 18.

_____ 3. A business operation that supplies illegal goods and services for profit.

_____ 4. Systematic practices developed by social groups to encourage conformity and to discourage deviance.

_____ 5. A behaviour that violates criminal law and is punishable with fines, jail terms, and other sanctions.

_____ 6. Circumstances that provide an opportunity for people to acquire through illegitimate activities what they cannot get through legitimate channels.

_____ 7. Deviants are those people who have been successfully labelled as such by others.

_____ 8. Illegal or unethical acts involving the misuse of power by government officials, or illegal/unethical acts by outsiders seeking to make a political statement, undermine the government, or overthrow it.

_____ 9. Any behaviour, belief, or condition that violates cultural norms.

_____ 10. Access to illegitimate opportunities.

_____ 11. Illegal acts committed by corporate employees on behalf of the corporation and with its support.

_____ 12. Offences such as robbery, assault, and break and enter.

_____ 13. Individuals have a greater tendency to deviate from societal norms when they frequently associate with persons who favour deviance over conformity.

_____ 14. Illegal activities committed by people in the course of their employment or financial dealings.

_____ 15. Women are exploited by capitalism and patriarchy.

_____ 16. Patriarchy keeps women more tied to family and home, even if women also work full-time.

_____ 17. People feel strain when they are exposed to cultural goals that they are unable to obtain because they do not have access to culturally approved means of achieving those goals.

_____ 18. A person who has been labelled a deviant accepts that new identity and continues the deviant behaviour.

_____ 19. The initial act of rule-breaking.

_____ 20. The criminal justice system protects the power and privilege of the capitalist class.

Key People

Margaret Beare (p. 187)   Edwin Lemert (p. 192)
Howard Becker (p. 191)   Robert Merton (p. 187)
William Chambliss (p. 191)   Walter Reckless (p. 189)
Richard Cloward & Lloyd Ohlin (p. 188)   Richard Quinney (p. 193)
Elizabeth Comack (p. 194)   Edwin Sutherland (p. 190)
Emile Durkheim (p. 186)   Daniel Wolf (p. 190)
Travis Hirschi (p. 189)

Review of Key People

_____ 1. Examined the relationship between women's earlier victimization in their family and their subsequent involvement in crime.

_____ 2. Suggest that for deviance to occur people must have access to illegitimate opportunity structures.

_____ 3. Defined primary and secondary deviance within a labelling theory.

_____ 4. Developed differential association theory to explain how people learn deviance through social interaction.

_____ 5. Has used Merton's strain theory to explain the increased involvement of Canadian Mohawks in the organized smuggling during the early 1990s.

_____ 6. Developed strain theory to explain how deviance results from the discrepancy between goals and the means to achieve them.

_____ 7. Described how a former Canadian penitentiary resident learned the art of safecracking.

_____ 8. Used labelling theory to explain how moral entrepreneurs use their own views of right and wrong to establish rules and label others as deviant.

_____ 9. Witnessed labelling theory in the response of law enforcement officials to two groups of high school boys (the "Saints" and the "Roughnecks").

_____ 10. An anthropologist who rode with the Rebels bike gang.

_____ 11. A functionalist who introduced the concept of anomie.

_____ 12. Developed a social bond theory of deviance that focuses on the elements of attachment, commitment, involvement, and belief.

_____ 13. According to this sociologist, people with economic and political power define as criminal any behaviour that threatens their own interests.

_____ 14. Developed a theory of social control that states that certain factors draw people toward deviance while others "insulate" them from such behaviour.

Learning Objectives

After reading Chapter 6, the student should be able to:

1. explain the nature of deviance and describe its most common forms (pp. 183-186).

2. identify the basic assumptions of strain theory (pp. 186-187).

3. identify the basic assumptions of opportunity theory (pp. 187-189).

4. identify the basic assumptions of control theory (p. 189).

5. describe the basic principles of differential association theory (p. 190).

6. describe the basic principles of labelling theory (pp. 190-192).

7. outline the key assumption of interactionist perspectives (pp. 189-190).

8. outline the key features of conflict perspectives on deviance (p. 192).

9. note the key strength and weakness of a critical approach to deviance and crime (pp. 192-193).

10. describe the three schools of feminist thought (pp. 193-194).

11. describe the kinds of behaviour included in street crimes (p. 194-197).

12. differentiate between occupational and corporate crime and explain why people who commit such crimes may not be viewed as "criminals" (pp. 197–198).

13. describe organized crime and political crime and explain how each may weaken social control in society (pp. 198–199).

14. explain how official crime statistics are obtained and why official statistics may not be an accurate reflection of the actual crimes committed (p. 199).

15. explain how victimization surveys and self-reports contribute to our understanding of crime in society (pp. 199-201).

16. describe the criminal justice system and explain how police, courts, and prisons have considerable discretion in dealing with offenders (pp. 205-209).

17. describe the five correlates of crime (i.e., state each correlate and provide a sentence that describes its relationship to crime) (pp. 201-205).

18. list and explain the four functions of punishment (pp. 207-209).

19. be able to distinguish between functional, interactionist, and conflict perspectives on deviance and crime (pp. 186-194).

Learning Objective Tests

Multiple Choice Questions

1. Who focuses on how people develop a self-concept and learn conforming behaviour through the process of socialization?
   a. feminists
   b. critical sociologists
   c. interactionists
   d. labelling theorists

2. According to conflict perspectives:
   a. people learn deviance through social interaction.
   b. people are drawn to deviance by poverty, unemployment, and lack of educational opportunity.
   c. strong bonds to society prevent people from becoming deviant.
   d. the law is used to protect the positions of those in power.

3. Which theory suggests that people must have access to illegitimate means before they can become criminal or deviant?
   a. conflict
   b. opportunity
   c. labelling
   d. critical

4. Which of the following theories claims that people get frustrated when they are subjected to cultural goals but do not have the means to achieve these goals?
   a. critical
   b. social control
   c. strain
   d. labelling

5. Which of the following statements is a valid criticism of the critical approach to deviance and crime?
   a. Critical theorists examine the relationship between class, race, and crime.
   b. People with economic and political power define as criminal any behaviour that threatens their own interests.
   c. People of all classes share a consensus about the criminality of certain acts.
   d. The poor commit street crimes in order to survive.

6. The idea that behaviour is not deviant in and of itself but, rather, is defined as such by a social audience forms the basis of which theory?
   a. differential association
   b. labelling
   c. feminism
   d. social control

7. A person who drinks too much or loses his or her rent money at a video lottery terminal would be considered:
   a. conventional.
   b. legitimate.
   c. criminal.
   d. deviant.

8. Which school of feminist thought argues that prostitution institutionalizes women's dependence on men and results in a form of female sexual slavery?
   a. radical feminism
   b. liberal feminism
   c. socialist feminism
   d. none of the above

9. The notion that deviant behaviour is minimal when people have strong bonds to families and other social institutions is central to which theory?
   a. strain
   b. labelling
   c. opportunity
   d. social control

10. Which of the following theories rests on the assumption that deviance is learned through social interaction?
    a. differential association
    b. strain
    c. social control
    d. labelling

11. Sexual assault and motor vehicle theft are classified as:
    a. conventional crimes.
    b. occupational crimes.
    c. corporate crimes.
    d. organized crimes.

12. Which of the following statements concerning official statistics is FALSE?
    a. Official statistics are generated from Canadian Uniform Crime Reports.
    b. Most public information comes from the Canadian Uniform Crime Reports.
    c. Police statistics always underreport the actual amount of crime.
    d. All crime statistics generated from Canadian Uniform Crime Reports are accurate.

13. An employee who overcharges customers for services in order to pocket the extra money has committed a(n):
    a. corporate crime.
    b. occupational crime.
    c. political crime.
    d. organized crime.

14. Which perspective focuses on the correspondence between culturally approved means and goals?
    a. functionalist
    b. interactionist
    c. feminist
    d. conflict

15. Why do the police have such a high degree of discretion in determining when charges will be laid?
    a. The police have a broad range of responsibilities.
    b. The police are one of the few public agencies open 24 hours a day.
    c. The police have the authority to intervene in situations where something must be done immediately.
    d. All of the above factors contribute to discretion in policing.

16. Which of the following is NOT one of the four functions of punishment?
    a. retribution
    b. rehabilitation
    c. restitution
    d. deterrence

17. Which of the following statements concerning major correlates of crime is TRUE?
    a. Aboriginal people are underrepresented in the criminal justice system.
    b. Arrest rates increase with age.
    c. Females are more likely to be offenders than victims.
    d. The age distribution for crime is remarkably stable.

18. Victimization surveys:
    a. often tell us about crimes that were never reported to the police.
    b. always underreport the actual amount of crime.
    c. clearly illustrate when crimes are on the increase.
    d. indicate that adolescents are most likely to break the law.

True–False Statements

TF   1. All societies have norms that govern acceptable behaviour (p. 183).

TF   2. As a result of high unemployment and lack of legitimate opportunities, many First Nation members turned to smuggling as a source of income (p. 187).

TF   3. Opportunity theory claims that the likelihood of deviant behaviour increases when ties to society are weakened or broken (pp. 187-188).

TF   4. Edwin Sutherland's (1939) differential association theory explains how deviance is learned through social interaction (p. 190).

TF   5. Primary deviance occurs when a person accepts the deviant label and continues the deviant behaviour (p. 192).

TF   6. From a conflict perspective, the law defines and controls persons who have been marginalized as well as members of stigmatized groups (p. 192).

TF   7. Liberal feminism explains women's deviance as a result of patriarchy, which keeps women more tied to family and home (p. 194).

TF   8. Corporate crime consists of illegal activities committed by people in the course of their employment or financial dealings (p. 197).

TF   9. Arrests increase from early adolescence, peak in young adulthood, and steadily decline with age (p. 201).

TF   10. Deterrence results from restricting offenders so they cannot commit further crimes (p. 207).

Fill-in-the-Blanks

1.   The _____ _____ _____ includes the police, the courts, and prisons (p. 205).

2.   _____ seeks to reduce criminal activity by instilling a fear of punishment (p. 207).

3.   Our most important source of crime data is the _____ _____ _____ _____ (p. 199).

4.   _____ _____ is a business operation that supplies illegal goods and services for profit (p. 198).

5.   According to _____ theory, two complementary processes are involved in the definition of deviance. First, some people act in a manner contrary to the expectation of others. Second, others disapprove of and try to control this behaviour (p. 190).

6.   According to Travis Hirschi (1969), social bonding consists of four elements: _____ to other people, _____ to conventional lines of behaviour such as schooling, _____ in conventional activities, and _____ in the legitimacy of conventional values (p. 189).

7.   Rule violations are dealt with through various mechanisms of _____ _____ , practices developed by social groups to encourage conformity and to discourage deviance (p. 183).

8.   Richard Cloward and Lloyd Ohlin (1960) have suggested that for deviance to occur people must have access to _____ _____ _____ (p. 187).

9.   People feel strain when they are exposed to cultural _____ that they are unable to obtain because they do not have access to culturally approved _____ (p. 186).

Matching Items

Match the concept with the appropriate theory about crime and deviance.

___ (a) social interaction   1. strain theory
___ (b) primary and secondary deviance   2. differential association theory
___ (c) cultural goals and means   3. labelling theory

Match the theory (or approach) to the appropriate theoretical perspective.

___ (a) labelling theory
___ (b) strain theory
___ (c) feminist approaches

1. functional perspective
2. interactionist perspective
3. conflict perspective

CHAPTER 7
SOCIAL STRATIFICATION AND CLASS

Chapter Outline

Chapter Summary

Social stratification is the hierarchical arrangement of large social groups based on their control over basic resources. A key characteristic of systems of stratification is the extent to which the structure is flexible. The **class system** is a type of stratification based on ownership of resources and on the type of work people do. Karl Marx and Max Weber identify social class as a key determinant of social inequality and change. According to Marx, capitalistic societies are comprised capitalists—who own the means of production—and workers—who sell their labour to the owners. Weber focuses on the interplay of **wealth, prestige,** and **power.** Functionalist perspectives on social stratification view classes as broad groupings of people who share similar levels of privilege based on the occupational structure. According to the Davis-Moore thesis, positions that are most important to society require the most talent and training and must be highly rewarded. Conflict perspectives assume that social stratification is created and maintained by the dominant group in order to protect its own economic interests. Stratification results in wide discrepancies in income, wealth, and access to available goods and services. **Absolute poverty** exists when people do not have the means to secure the basic necessities of life, and **relative poverty** exists when people may be able to afford basic necessities but are still unable to maintain an average standard of living. There are both economic and structural sources of poverty. Low wages are a key problem, as are unemployment and underemployment. If we do nothing, the gap between rich and poor, employed and unemployed, will widen and social inequality will increase in the 21st century.

Key Terms

absolute poverty (p. 233)
apartheid (p. 218)
caste system (p. 218)
class system (p. 220)
feminization of poverty (p. 235)
intergenerational mobility (p. 217)
intragenerational mobility (p. 217)
job deskilling (p. 238)
life chances (p. 216)

meritocracy (p. 224)
power (p. 222)
proletariat (p. 221)
prestige (p. 222)
relative poverty (p. 234)
social mobility (p. 217)
social stratification (p. 216)
socioeconomic status (SES) (p. 227)
wealth (p. 222)

Review of Key Terms

_____ 1. A combined measure that attempts to classify individuals, families, or households in terms of indicators such as income, occupation, and education to determine class location.

_____ 2. Relatively low-paying, nonmanual, semiskilled positions primarily held by women such as daycare workers, checkout clerks, etc.

_____ 3. Exists when people do not have the means to secure the most basic necessities of life.

_____ 4. Exists when people may be able to afford basic necessities but still are unable to maintain an average standard of living.

_____ 5. A reduction in the proficiency needed to perform a specific job that leads to a corresponding reduction in the wages for that job.

_____ 6. A hierarchy in which all positions are rewarded based on people's ability and credentials.

_____ 7. The movement of individuals or groups from one level in a stratification system to another.

_____ 8. The social movement experienced by family members from one generation to the next.

_____ 9. The social movement of individuals within their own lifetime.

_____ 10. Describes the extent to which persons within a particular layer of stratification have access to important scarce resources.

_____ 11. The separation of the races.

_____ 12. A type of stratification based on the ownership and control of resources and on the type of work people do.

_____ 13. A system of social inequality in which people's status is permanently determined at birth based on their parents' ascribed characteristics.

_____ 14. The value of all of a person's or family's economic assets, including income, personal property, and income-producing property.

_____ 15. The ability of people or groups to achieve their goals despite opposition from others.

_____ 16. The respect with which a person or status position is regarded by others.

_____ 17. Refers to the trend in which women are disproportionately represented among individuals living in poverty.

_____ 18. Refers to the persistent patterns of social inequality within a society, perpetuated by the manner in which wealth, power, and prestige are distributed and passed on from one generation to the next.

Key People

Gerhard Lenski (p. 225)   Diana Pearce (p. 235)
Karl Marx (p. 220)   Max Weber (p. 222)
Kingsley Davis and Wilbert Moore (p. 223)

Review of Key People

_____ 1. Developed a structural functional theory of social stratification.

_____ 2. Coined the term "feminization of poverty" and explained why women have a higher risk of being poor.

_____ 3. Argued that class position is determined by people's relationship to the means of production.

_____ 4. Developed a multidimensional approach to social stratification that focused on the interplay among wealth, prestige, and power.

_____ 5. Developed an evolutionary approach to explain social stratification and inequality as a function of power and privilege.

Learning Objectives

After reading Chapter 7, students should be able to:

1. define social stratification and describe the major sources of stratification found in societies (pp. 216-217).

2. explain social mobility and distinguish between intergenerational and intragenerational mobility (pp. 217-218).

3. describe the key characteristics of the two major systems of stratification (pp. 217-220).

4. describe Karl Marx's perspective on class position and class relationships (pp. 220-222).

5. outline Max Weber's multidimensional approach to social stratification and explain how people are ranked on all three dimensions (pp. 222-223).

6. compare functionalist and conflict approaches to social stratification (pp. 223-225).

7. outline Davis and Moore's explanation of why social stratification exists in Canadian society (pp. 223-225).

8. outline the evolutionary model of social stratification and explain how the nature of social stratification varies from one type of society to another (pp. 225-226).

9. outline the Canadian class structure (pp. 227).

10. discuss the distribution of income in Canada (p. 229).

11. understand how wealth is distributed in Canada and outline how this distribution affects life chances (pp. 229-230).

12. outline some of the key consequences of inequality for health and nutritionin Canada (pp. 230-233).

13. explain how inequalities in wealth and income affect educational opportunities (p. 233).

14. distinguish between absolute and relative poverty (p. 233-234).

15. describe the characteristics and lifestyle of those who live in poverty in Canada (pp. 233-237).

16. describe the feminization of poverty and explain why two out of three impoverished adults in Canada are women (pp. 234-236).

17. list and describe the key recommendations made by the National Council of Welfare for addressing the issue of poverty in Canada (pp. 238-240).

Learning Objective Tests

Multiple Choice Questions

1. What type of social stratification system is based on occupation, in which families typically perform the same type of work from generation to generation?
    a. superstructure
    b. open system
    c. class system
    d. caste system

2. All of the following statements about social stratification are true EXCEPT:
    a. Social stratification involves patterns of inequality.
    b. Social stratification is absent from some societies.
    c. Social stratification exists in Canada.
    d. The distribution of wealth, power, and prestige perpetuates social stratification.

3. Which approach to social stratification identifies ownership or nonownership of the means of production as the distinguishing feature of classes?
    a. evolutionary
    b. feminist
    c. functional
    d. conflict

4. Suppose you have adequate food and clothing, but you feel poor because your children have fewer toys than do other children in the neighbourhood. This demonstrates:
    a. absolute poverty.
    b. relative poverty.
    c. substandard poverty.
    d. relational poverty.

5. Women have a high risk of being poor because:
    a. they bear the major economic burden of raising children.
    b. many are unable to obtain regular, full-time, year-round employment.
    c. of events such as marital separation, divorce, and widowhood.
    d. all of the above increase women's risk of being poor.

6. For Karl Marx, class position is determined by:
    a. people's relationship to the means of production.
    b. the most important positions being filled by the most qualified individuals.
    c. the value of economic assets.
    d. opportunities for advancement within a stratification system.

7. There are _____ broad social classes in Canada.
   a. two
   b. three
   c. four
   d. five

8. Suppose someone progresses from an extended period of unemployment to obtaining a college degree to securing a modest income in a fairly prestigious occupation. That person has experienced:
   a. intergenerational mobility.
   b. intragenerational mobility.
   c. a closed system.
   d. ascribed status.

9. Which of the following statements about wealth and health is TRUE?
   a. Children born into poor families have the same risk of dying in their first year as middle-class babies.
   b. The poor have shorter life expectancies than other social classes.
   c. Most poor people receive adequate medical care following illness or injury.
   d. Most high-poverty areas have an adequate supply of doctors and medical facilities.

10. According to functionalists, which of the following statements about the education system is TRUE?
    a. The education system is inflexible.
    b. Inequality in education is increasing.
    c. Class, race, and gender are more important to life chances than student ability.
    d. Educational opportunities and life chances are directly linked.

11. Which of the following is NOT a National Council of Welfare recommendation for solving the poverty problem?
    a. Governments should increase taxes so that everyone, including the poor, pay their share in deficit reduction.
    b. Governments should agree to work collectively to fight poverty.
    c. Governments should make a special effort to promote realistic portraits of poor people.
    d. Governments should add fighting poverty to their list of immediate economic priorities.

12. Which of the following statements accurately depicts the income distribution in Canada?
    a. The wealthiest 20 percent of households receive over 40 percent of the total income.
    b. The poorest 20 percent of households receive about 20 percent of the total income.
    c. The top 10 percent receive 40 percent of all income.
    d. The top 10 percent receive 60 percent of all income.

13. Max Weber's multidimensional approach to social stratification focused on the interplay among all of the following elements EXCEPT:
    a. wealth.
    b. power.
    c. educational attainment.
    d. prestige.

14. Which of the following statements accurately summarizes the Davis–Moore thesis of social stratification?
    a. Some positions are more important for the survival of society than others.
    b. The most important positions must be filled by the most qualified people.
    c. The positions that are most important require scarce talent or extensive training and thus should be the most highly rewarded.
    d. all of the above are central to the Davis–Moore thesis.

15. Wealth includes all of the following EXCEPT:
    a. income.
    b. property.
    c. corporate stocks, bonds, and insurance policies.
    d. all of the above make up wealth.

16. Who is most likely to be poor in Canada?
    a. an elderly male
    b. an elderly female
    c. a white elderly person
    d. a native child

17. Who developed an evolutionary approach to social stratification based on power and privilege?
    a. Gerhard Lenski
    b. Karl Marx
    c. Kingsley Davis and Wilbert Moore
    d. Max Weber

True–False Statements

TF   1.   An ascribed status is a changeable status depending on how well an individual performs in a particular role (p. 216).

TF   2.   Social stratification in one form or another exists in all societies (p. 216).

TF   3.   Intergenerational mobility is a social movement within one's lifetime (p. 217).

TF   4.   In a class system, people are allowed to marry only within their own group (p. 220).

TF   5.   The interplay between wealth, power, and prestige determines people's location in the class structure (p. 222).

TF   6.   People may have prestige but not wealth (p. 222).

TF   7.   Hunting and gathering societies are highly stratified with marked differences in property, power, and prestige (p. 225).

TF   8.   An important contribution of the Davis–Moore thesis is that it directs attention to the distribution of social prestige based on occupation (p. 223).

TF   9.   Functionalist approaches claim that inequality results from the more powerful exploiting the less powerful (p. 223).

Fill-in-the-Blanks

1.   _____ is a closed system of social stratification (p. 218).

2.   Wealth, prestige, and _____ are separate continuums on which people can be ranked from high to low (p. 222).

3.   The _____ - _____ thesis assumes that social stratification results in meritocracy (p. 223).

4.   Fame, respect, honour, and esteem are the most common forms of _____ (p. 222).

5.   Social _____ in modern societies is held by bureaucracies (p. 222).

6.   _____ theory is based on the assumption that social stratification is created and maintained by one group in order to protect and enhance its own economic interests (p. 224).

7.   _____ is the economic gain derived from wages, salaries, social assistance, and ownership of property (p. 229).

8.   _____ includes property such as buildings, farms, houses, and other assets (p. 229).

9.   _____ _____ describes the reduction in the proficiency needed to perform a specific job that goes along with lower wages (p. 238).

Matching Items

<u>1. Match the theorist with the appropriate concept.</u>

___ (a) Gerhard Lenski   1. feminization of poverty
___ (b) Kingsley Davis and Wilbert Moore   2. evolution of social stratification
___ (c) Diana Pearce   3. meritocracy

CHAPTER 8
RACE AND ETHNICITY

Chapter Outline

Race and Ethnicity
>   Social Significance of Race and Ethnicity
>   Majority and Minority Groups

Components of Racial and Ethnic Conflict
>   Prejudice
>   Discrimination
>   Racism

Theories of Prejudice, Discrimination, and Racism
Patterns of Interaction between Racial and Ethnic Groups
Ethnic Groups in Canada
>   First Nations
>   Charter Europeans
>   Canada's Immigrants

Racial and Ethnic Diversity in Canada in the 21st Century

Chapter Summary

Issues of race and ethnicity permeate all levels of interaction in Canada. A **race** is a category of people who have been singled out as inferior or superior, often on the basis of physical characteristics such as skin colour, hair texture, and eye shape. By contrast, an **ethnic group** is a collection of people who, as a result of their shared cultural traits and a high level of interaction, are regarded as a cultural unit. Race and ethnicity are ingrained in our consciousness and often form the basis of hierarchical ranking and determine who gets what resources. A **majority** (or dominant) group is one that is advantaged and has superior resources and rights in a society, while a **minority** (or subordinate) group is one whose members, because of physical or cultural characteristics, are disadvantaged and subjected to unequal treatment by the dominant group and who regard themselves as objects of collective discrimination. **Prejudice** is a negative attitude based on preconceived notions about the members of selected racial and ethnic groups. **Discrimination**—actions or practices of dominant group members that have a harmful impact on members of a subordinate group—may be either **de jure** (encoded in law) or **de facto** (involving informal discrimination that is entrenched in the social customs and day-to-day practices of organizations and institutions). **Racism** is an organized set of beliefs about the innate inferiority of some racial groups, combined with the power to transform these ideas into practices that deny equality on the basis of race. Racism involves elements of prejudice, discrimination, ethnocentrism, and stereotyping, and takes many different forms, including rednecked racism, polite racism, subliminal racism, and institutionalized racism. The unique experiences of native peoples, white Anglo-Saxon

Protestants/British Canadians, French Canadians, and Canada's immigrant population are discussed, and the increasing racial/ethnic diversity of Canada is examined.

Key Terms

assimilation (p. 260)
authoritarian personality (p. 258)
discrimination (p. 252)
ethnic group (p. 247)
ethnic pluralism (p. 260)
ethnocentrism (p. 252)
genocide (p. 263)
institutionalized racism (p. 255)
internal colonialism (p. 262)
majority (dominant) group (p. 251)
minority (subordinate) group (p. 251)

polite racism (p. 254)
prejudice (p. 251)
race (p. 246)
racial prejudice (p. 252)
racism (p. 254)
scapegoat (p. 258)
segregation (p. 263)
social distance (p. 258)
split labour market (p. 259)
systemic racism (p. 256)

Review of Key Terms

_____ 1. A category of people who have been singled out as inferior as a result of physical characteristics.

_____ 2. A person or group that is incapable of offering resistance to the hostility or aggression of others.

_____ 3. A process by which members of a subordinate racial or ethnic group become absorbed into the dominant culture.

_____ 4. Characterized by excessive conformity, intolerance, a propensity for stereotyping, and rigid thinking.

_____ 5. An attempt to disguise a dislike of others through behaviour that appears to be nonprejudicial.

_____ 6. A negative attitude based on preconceived notions about members of selected groups.

_____ 7. Made up of the rules, procedures, and practices that directly and deliberately prevent minorities from having full and equal involvement in society.

_____ 8. Involves actions or practices of dominant group members that have a harmful impact on members of a subordinate group.

_____ 9. An organized set of beliefs about the innate inferiority of some racial groups, combined with the power to transform these beliefs into practices that deny equality of treatment on the basis of race.

_____ 10. The deliberate, systematic killing of an entire people or nation.

_____ 11. A collection of people who, as a result of their shared cultural traits and a high level of interaction, regard themselves and are regarded as a cultural unit.

_____ 12. The coexistence of a variety of distinct racial and ethnic groups in society.

_____ 13. A situation in which members of a racial or ethnic group are conquered or colonized and forcibly placed under the economic and political control of the dominant group.

_____ 14. Refers to the division of the economy into two areas of employment—an upper tier of higher-paid workers and a lower tier of subordinate workers who are paid considerably less.

_____ 15. The extent to which people are willing to interact and establish relationships with members of racial and ethnic groups other than their own.

_____ 16. The spatial and social separation of categories of people by race, ethnicity, class, gender, and/or religion.

_____ 17. A group that is advantaged and has superior resources and rights in a society.

_____ 18. A group that is disadvantaged relative to the dominant group as a result of physical or cultural characteristics.

Key People

Theodore W. Adorno (p. 330)
Emory Bogardus (p. 331)

Augie Fleras and
Jean Leonard Elliott (p. 319)
John Porter (p. 320)

Review of Key People

_____ 1. Wrote a book titled *Is God a Racist? The Right Wing in Canada,* which discusses racism among the elite.

_____ 2. Studied the effects of culturally rooted prejudices on interpersonal relationships and developed the concept of social distance to measure levels of prejudice.

_____ 3. Described Canada as a "vertical mosaic."

_____ 4. Claimed that prejudiced people often have an authoritarian personality.

_____ 5. Developed a typology of prejudice and discriminatory types.

_____ 6. Described segregation of blacks in Northern Ontario.

_____ 7. Described the significance of the "white privilege."

Learning Objectives

After reading Chapter 8, the student should be able to:

1. define race and ethnicity and explain their social significance (pp. 246-249).

2. explain the sociological usage of majority group and minority group and note why these terms may be misleading (p. 251).

3. define prejudice and list some of the social or personal characteristics it may be directed against (pp. 251-252).

4. define discrimination and distinguish between *de jure* and *de facto* discrimination (pp. 252-254).

5. identify and explain the different types of racism (pp. 254-257).

6. outline the key assumptions of the scapegoat theory of prejudice (pp. 257-258).

7. describe how social learning is implicated in prejudice (p. 258).

8. list the key characteristics of an authoritarian personality (p. 258).

9. describe how a cultural theory explains prejudice and provide evidence of support for this theory (pp. 258-259).

10. explain the key assumptions of conflict perspectives on racial and ethnic relations (pp. 259-260).

11. define assimilation and discuss how assimilation occurs at several distinct levels (p. 260).

12. distinguish between ethnic pluralism and internal colonialism (pp. 260-262).

13. define segregation and explain the significance of the Jim Crow laws in the Southern United States (pp. 262-263).

14. define genocide and indicate the conditions in which it is likely to occur (p. 263).

15. be able to distinguish between the intergroup relationships dealt with in learning objectives 11–14 (pp. 260-263).

16. explain how the experiences of First Nations peoples have been different from those of other racial and ethnic groups in Canada (pp. 263-266).

17. describe how the French Canadian experience in Canada has been unique when compared with other groups (pp. 267-268).

18. compare and contrast the experiences of Chinese, Japanese, East Indian, and Jewish Canadians (pp. 268-270).

19. discuss major immigration trends from 1929 to present (p. 270).

20. discuss the impact of racial and ethnic diversity in the 21st century (pp. 270-272).

Learning Objective Tests

Multiple Choice Questions

1. Which of the following statements about Canada's native people is CORRECT?
   a. Native people are the most advantaged racial and ethnic group in Canada.
   b. Native people constitute an extremely homogenous group.
   c. Native people have been victims of genocide and forced migration.
   d. The Indian Act of 1876 protected the values, customs, and languages of native people.

2. The killing of thousands of native Americans by white settlers in North America demonstrates:
   a. genocide.
   b. pluralism.
   c. apartheid.
   d. assimilation.

3. Changes to the Immigration Act in 1962:
   a. sent many Japanese Canadians back to Japan.
   b. allowed East Indians to immigrate only if they came directly from India and did not stop at any port along the way.
   c. gave immigrants from Britain preferential treatment.
   d. opened the door to immigration on a nonracial basis.

4. Beliefs that certain racial groups are innately inferior to others form the basis of:
   a. ethnocentrism.
   b. racial prejudice.
   c. discrimination.
   d. none of the above.

5. Which theory claims that prejudice is the end result of a frustration–aggression process?
   a. scapegoat theory
   b. social learning
   c. cultural theory
   d. authoritarian personality

6. Which of the following statements concerning French Canadians is FALSE?
   a. The British North America Act formally acknowledged the rights and privileges of the French and British as the founding groups of Canadian society.
   b. The French conquered the British in the Seven Year War, rendering Canada a French dominion.
   c. Bill 101 established French as the sole official language in Quebec.
   d. Today approximately 25 percent of the Canadian population is francophone.

7. A(n) _____ group is defined by shared cultural traits and a high level of interaction.
   a. racial
   b. ethnic
   c. majority
   d. minority

8. All of the following are considered a minority group EXCEPT:
   a. Chinese.
   b. white women.
   c. blacks.
   d. all of the above are considered minority members.

9. Most Canadians, whatever their ethnic origin, have a positive perception and attitude toward French and English Canadians. This supports a:
   a. split labour theory of prejudice.
   b. scapegoat theory of prejudice.
   c. social learning theory of prejudice.
   d. cultural theory of prejudice.

10. Which of the following statements about Canada's immigrants is FALSE?
    a. Chinese immigrants did not experience prejudice because they were recruited to work on the railway.
    b. Jewish Canadians today have a considerably higher level of education and income relative to the average Canadian.
    c. During World War II, people of Japanese ancestry were placed in internment camps because they were seen as a security threat.
    d. East Indians were denied citizenship and the right to vote in British Columbia until 1947.

11. In Nova Scotia, New Brunswick, and Ontario, blacks were once set apart from whites, resulting in unequal access to power and privilege in schools, government, and the workplace. This is called:
    a. structural assimilation.
    b. cultural assimilation.
    c. ethnic pluralism.
    d. segregation.

12. All of the following are major patterns of interaction between racial and ethnic groups EXCEPT:
    a. assimilation.
    b. ethnic pluralism.
    c. social learning.
    d. internal colonization.

13. All of the following are patterns of interaction that develop between racial and ethnic groups EXCEPT:
    a. assimilation.
    b. immigration.
    c. ethnic pluralism.
    d. internal colonialism.

14. What type of discrimination is backed by explicit laws?
    a. rednecked racism
    b. institutionalized racism
    c. de facto
    d. de jure

15. Theodore W. Adorno claimed that highly prejudiced individuals tend to:
    a. have prejudiced parents.
    b. have an authoritarian personality.
    c. engage in police racism.
    d. promote subliminal racism.

16. White workers in the upper tier of the employment sector who use racial discrimination against nonwhites to protect their positions illustrate:
    a. the authoritarian personality theory
    b. the split labour market theory
    c. de jure discrimination
    d. internal colonialization

17. Which of the following is an accurate prediction of racial and ethnic diversity for the 21st century?
    a. Racial and ethnic diversity is diminishing.
    b. There will be no racial and ethnic diversity in the 21st century.
    c. Canada is becoming more ethnically and racially diverse.
    d. Canada is racially but not ethnically diverse.

18. A situation in which many groups share elements of the mainstream culture while remaining culturally distinct from the dominant group is:
    a. apartheid.
    b. cultural assimilation.
    c. ethnic pluralism.
    d. internal colonialism.

19. An ethnic group adopts the language, dress, values, and religion of the dominant group. This is an example of:
    a. structural assimilation.
    b. acculturation.
    c. amalgamation.
    d. psychological assimilation.

20. According to social learning theorists, prejudice results from:
    a. observing and imitating significant others such as parents and peers.
    b. social distance in specific situations.
    c. excessive conformity and rigid thinking.
    d. frustration in the effort to achieve a goal.

True–False Statements

TF   1. Race refers to cultural features such as language, religion, and distinctive dress (p. 247).

TF   2. A significant degree of ethnic stratification exists in society (pp. 250-251).

TF   3. A minority group has superior resources and rights in a society (p. 251).

TF   4. By choice or by necessity, members of minority groups usually marry within the group (p. 251).

TF   5. Prejudice is often reinforced by stereotypes (pp. 251-252).

TF   6. Discrimination involves differential treatment based on irrelevant characteristics such as skin colour and language preference (pp. 252-254).

TF   7. For many Canadians, the media are a primary source of information about racial and ethnic groups (p. 253).

TF   8. Polite racism involves unconscious criticism of minorities (p. 254).

TF   9. Systemic racism is conscious, personal, and explicit (p. 256).

TF　　10. Racism involves elements of prejudice, ethnocentrism, stereotyping, and discrimination (p. 254).

Fill-in-the-Blanks

1. Enjoying the benefits that go along with being part of the dominant white group has been referred to as the _____ _____ (p. 250).

2. The term _____ _____ refers to an official government category of nonwhite non-Caucasian individuals (p. 251).

3. _____ involves the evaluation of all groups and cultures in terms of one's own cultural standards and values (p. 252).

4. _____ racism is entrenched in the structure, function, and process of many social institutions (p. 256).

5. According to the split labour market theory, white workers in the _____ _____ may use racial discrimination against nonwhite to protect their positions (p. 259).

6. _____ _____ occurs when members of an ethnic group adopt dominant group traits, such as language or dress (p. 260).

7. _____ _____ occurs when members of subordinate racial or ethnic groups gain acceptance in everyday social interaction with members of the dominant group (p. 260).

8. _____ exists when specific ethnic groups are set apart from the dominant groups and have unequal access to power and privilege (pp. 262-263).

Matching Items

1. Match the theory of prejudice with its key assumption.

____ (a) scapegoat
____ (b) social learning
____ (c) authoritarian personality
____ (d) cultural

1. excessively conforming traits
2. observing and imitating significant others
3. built-in prejudices in favour of charter groups
4. basis in frustration and aggression

2. Match the pattern of interaction to its key feature.

___ (a) assimilation
___ (b) ethnic pluralism
___ (c) segregation
___ (d) internal colonialism
___ (e) genocide

1. coexistence of many ethnic groups
2. conquering of racial or ethnic groups
3. spatial and social separation of categories
4. abolishment of an entire race or ethnicity
5. absorption of subordinate groups

CHAPTER 9
SEX AND GENDER

Chapter Outline

Sex and Gender
  Sex
  Gender
  The Social Significance of Gender
  Sexism
Gender Stratification in Historical Perspective
  Hunting and Gathering Societies
  Horticultural and Pastoral Societies
  Agrarian Societies
  Industrial Societies
Gender and Socialization
  Gender Socialization by Parents
  Peers and Gender Socialization
  Teachers and Schools and Gender Socialization
  Mass Media and Gender Socialization
  Adult Gender Socialization
Contemporary Gender Inequality
  Gendered Division of Paid Work
  Pay Equity and Employment Equity
  Paid Work and Family Work
Perspectives on Gender Stratification
  Functionalist and Neoclassical Economic Perspectives
  Conflict Perspectives
  Feminist Perspectives
Gender Issues in the 21st Century

Chapter Summary

It is important to distinguish between **sex**—the biological and anatomical differences between females and males—and **gender**—the socially constructed differences between females and males found in the meanings, beliefs, and practices associated with "femininity" and "masculinity." Sexism (the differential treatment of women and men) is linked to patriarchy, a hierarchical system in which cultural, political, and economic structures are male dominated. In industrialized societies, a gap exists between unpaid work performed by women at home and paid work performed by men and women. The key agents of gender socialization are parents, peers, teachers and schools, sports, and the mass media, all of which tend to reinforce gender stereotypes. Gender inequality results from the economic, political, and educational discrimination of women.

In most workplaces, jobs are either gender segregated or the majority of employees are of the same gender. Even when women are employed in the same job as men, on average they do not receive the same, or comparable, pay. According to functional analysts, husbands perform instrumental tasks of economic support and decision making, and wives assume expressive tasks of providing affection and emotional support for the family. Conflict analysts suggest that the gendered division of labour within families and the workplace results from male control and dominance over women and resources. Feminist perspectives advocate social change to eradicate gender inequality.

Key Terms

body consciousness (p. 283)	pay equity (p. 300)
employment equity (p. 301)	primary sex characteristics (p. 280)
feminism (p. 305)	secondary sex characteristics (p. 280)
gender (p. 282	sex (p. 280)
gender bias (p. 295)	sexism (p. 285)
gender identity (p. 283)	sexual orientation (p. 281)
gender role (p. 283)	transsexual (p. 282)
hermaphrodite (p. 282)	transvestite (p. 282)
matriarchy (p. 285)	wage gap (p. 299)
patriarchy (p. 285)	

Review of Key Terms

_____ 1. The belief that women and men are equal and that they should be valued equally and have equal rights.

_____ 2. The biological and anatomical differences between females and males.

_____ 3. The subordination of one sex, usually female, based on the assumed superiority of the other sex.

_____ 4. A person who believes that he or she was born with the body of the wrong sex.

_____ 5. Consists of showing favouritism toward one gender over another.

_____ 6. A hierarchical system of social organization in which cultural, political, and economic structures are controlled by men.

_____ 7. A hierarchical system of social organization in which cultural, political, and economic structures are controlled by women.

_____ 8. A person in whom sexual differentiation is ambiguous or incomplete.

_____ 9. How a person perceives and feels about his or her body.

_____ 10. The culturally and socially constructed differences between females and males found in the meanings, beliefs, and practices associated with "femininity" and "masculinity."

_____ 11. Refers to the attitudes, behaviour, and activities that are socially defined as appropriate for each sex and are learned through the socialization process.

_____ 12. A person's perception of the self as female or male.

_____ 13. A preference for emotional–sexual relationships with members of the opposite sex, the same sex, or both sexes.

_____ 14. A male who lives as a woman or a female who lives as a man but does not alter the genitalia.

_____ 15. The genitalia used in the reproductive process.

_____ 16. The physical traits (other than reproductive organs) that identify an individual's sex.

_____ 17. Is the policy according to which wages are to reflect the worth of a job, not the gender or race of the worker.

_____ 18. A term referring to the disparity between women's and men's earnings.

Key People

Ben Agger (p. 305)   Arlie Hochschild (p. 303)
George F. Gilder (p. 304)   Jean Kilbourne (p. 297)
Dorothy C. Holland and   Judith Lorber (p. 283)
    Margaret A. Eisenhart (p. 294)   Myra Sadker and David Sadker (p. 295)

Review of Key People

_____ 1. Found that advertisements directed at women emphasize the need for diet products and a fear of being fat.

_____ 2. Claimed that sports illustrate the ways bodies are gendered by social practices and how the female body is socially constructed to be inferior.

_____ 3. Found that working mothers talked about sleep the way a hungry person talks about food.

_____ 4. Argued that traditional gender roles are important.

_____ 5. Found that the peer system propelled women into a world of romance in which their attractiveness to men counted most.

_____ 6. Asserts that relationships between men and women are damaged when changes in gender roles occur, and family life suffers as a consequence.

_____ 7. Found that teachers consistently devote more time to boys than to girls.

Learning Objectives

After reading Chapter 9, the student should be able to:

1. define sex and distinguish between primary and secondary sex characteristics (p. 280).

2. explain why sex is not always clear-cut; differentiate between hermaphrodites, transsexuals, and transvestites (p. 282).

3. define gender and explain its social significance (pp. 282-285).

4. describe the relationship between gender roles and gender identity (p. 283).

5. explain how body consciousness is related to gender identity (pp. 283-284).

6. describe how eating disorders and body building illustrate the social significance of gender (pp. 284-285).

7. define sexism and explain how it is related to discrimination and patriarchy (pp. 285-287).

8. explain how gender stratification in hunting and gathering societies differs from horticultural and pastoral societies (pp. 287-288).

9. outline the similarities in gender stratification between agrarian and industrialized societies (pp. 288-292).

10. describe the process of gender socialization and identify specific ways in which parents and peers contribute to this process (pp. 292-294).

11. describe gender bias and explain how schools operate as a gendered institution (pp. 294-295).

12. explain how the mass media contribute to gender socialization (pp. 295-298).

13. discuss the gendered division of paid work (pp. 298-299).

14. explain what pay equity is and how you determine if pay discrimination exists (pp. 299-302).

15. trace changes in the labour force participation by women and note how these changes have contributed to a "second shift" (pp. 302-303).

16. describe functionalist and neoclassical economic perspectives (pp. 303-304).

17. outline the key assumptions of liberal, radical, and socialist perspectives on gender equality (pp. 305-306).

18. list the key trends in gender issues expected for the 21st century (pp. 307-308).

Learning Objective Tests

Multiple Choice Questions

1. A hermaphrodite is a person who:
    a. believes that he or she was born with the body of the wrong sex.
    b. has a sexual preference for members of the opposite sex.
    c. has some combination of male and female genitals.
    d. behaves and dresses like a women but is really a man.

2. Which of the following statements best explains the social significance of excessive dieting and body building?
    a. Compulsive dieting and body building result in the formation of hermaphrodites.
    b. Gender is absent from dieting and body building.
    c. Dieting and body building helps eliminate gender stereotypes.
    d. The body is objectified in both compulsive dieting and body building.

3. Which of the following statements accurately describes the similarity between agrarian and industrialized societies?
    a. Men control procreation and women's status is low.
    b. Women control procreation and women's status is high.
    c. Men and women have equal status and control over procreation.
    d. Inheritance is shared and women's status is high.

4. Which of the following statements about gender socialization is FALSE?
    a. From birth, parents act toward children on the basis of the child's sex.
    b. Peers help children learn prevailing gender stereotypes.
    c. Peers help children learn gender inappropriate behaviour.
    d. Female peer groups put more pressure on girls to do feminine things than male peer groups place on boys.

5. That media involve gender socialization is evident in:
    a. the fact that men outnumber women as leading characters.
    b. the fact that cartoons and adult shows are sex typed and white-male oriented.
    c. advertising messages to embrace traditional notions of masculinity and femininity as a means of gaining social success.
    d. All of the above are examples of mass-media gender socialization.

6. Which of the following statements about the gendered division of paid work in Canada is FALSE?
    a. Women remain concentrated in lower-paying traditionally female jobs.
    b. The workplace is an example of a gendered institution.
    c. There is no gender segregation in the workplace.
    d. Gender segregated work has a negative effect on men and women.

7.   All of the following are criticisms of functionalist perspectives on gender EXCEPT:
     a.   Traditional gender roles result in strains for men and women.
     b.   Men might prefer to spend more time in child-rearing activities.
     c.   Women may prefer to spend time in the workplace over the home.
     d.   All of the above are criticisms of the functionalist perspective.

8.   All of the following are anticipated gender trends for the 21st century EXCEPT:
     a.   The pay gap between men and women should continue to decrease.
     b.   Gender segregation may increase if the number of female-dominated jobs continues to grow.
     c.   Many men will continue to join movements to raise consciousness about men's concerns.
     d.   Affirmative action policies will be prohibited.

9.   Biological attributes of men and women are referred to as:
     a.   gender.
     b.   sex.
     c.   sexual orientation.
     d.   sexism.

10. Social and cultural processes, not biological "givens," are most important in defining what females and males are and what they should do. This argument favours:
     a.   gender.
     b.   sex.
     c.   sexual orientation.
     d.   sexism.

11. Being small and weak as a male often results in disapproval of others. This illustrates:
     a.   patriarchy.
     b.   sexism.
     c.   sexual orientation.
     d.   body consciousness.

12. Which of the following statements about horticultural and pastoral societies is TRUE?
     a.   Inheritance is partrilineal.
     b.   Women's status is very low.
     c.   Men own the means of production and control procreation.
     d.   Men begin to control societies and women's status is decreasing.

13. In which form of feminism is gender equality equated with equality of opportunity?
    a. radical feminism
    b. liberal feminism
    c. socialist feminism
    d. neofeminism

14. The term "second shift" is generally used to refer to:
    a. additional unpaid hours worked by employees who have little job security.
    b. having to work a part-time job along with a full-time one to make ends meet.
    c. the dual responsibilities that females face in terms of paid employment in conjunction with childcare and housework.
    d. time segregation in the workplace.

15. The belief that wages ought to reflect the worth of a job, not the gender or race of the worker, is known as:
    a. pay equity.
    b. wage gap.
    c. sexism.
    d. employment equity.

16. Sexism directed at women contains all of the following elements EXCEPT:
    a. negative attitudes toward women.
    b. stereotypical beliefs that reinforce, complement, or justify the prejudice.
    c. sexual orientation.
    d. discrimination.

17. Which of the following statements about gender identity is FALSE?
    a. Gender identity concerns one's perception of the self as a male or female.
    b. Gender identity is established by the time a person reaches 3 years of age.
    c. Gender identity includes behaviours and activities that are socially defined as appropriate for each sex.
    d. Most people form a gender identification that matches their biological sex.

18. Which of the following statements about gender socialization by teachers and schools is FALSE?
    a. Most fields of study retain a male or female orientation.
    b. Teacher–student interactions influence not only students' learning but also their self-esteem.
    c. Studies show that one of the messages that teachers may communicate is that girls are more important than boys.
    d. The content of teacher–student interaction is very important.

True–False Statements

TF   1.   At birth, male and female infants are distinguished by secondary sex characteristics (p. 280).

TF   2.   Western societies acknowledge the existence of only two sexes (p. 282).

TF   3.   Body consciousness is a part of gender identity (p. 283).

TF   4.   A transsexual believes that he or she was born with the body of the wrong sex (p. 282).

TF   5.   Gender is a social construction with important consequences in every day (p. 284).

TF   6.   In Canadian society, males traditionally are expected to demonstrate aggressiveness and toughness while females are expected to be passive and nurturing (p. 283).

TF   7.   At conception, the father contributes an X chromosome and the mother either an X or Y chromosome (p. 280).

TF   8.   Gender identity is typically established between 18 months and 3 years of age (p. 283).

TF   9.   Even with dramatic changes in women's workforce participation, the sexual division of labour in the family remains essentially unchanged (p. 302).

TF   10.   According to radical feminists, male domination causes all forms of human oppression (p. 306).

Fill-in-the-Blanks

1.   At puberty, an increased production of hormones results in the development of ____ ____ ____ (p. 280).

2.   _____ tend to have some combination of male and female genitalia (p. 282).

3.   A _____ is genetically of one sex but has a gender identity of the other sex (p. 282).

4.   Structural features that perpetuate gender inequality are referred to as ____ ____ (p. 283).

5. _____ _____ or comparable worth is the idea that wages should correspond to the worth of a job, not the gender, of the worker (p. 300).

6. In Canadian society, males are expected to demonstrate aggressiveness and toughness as part of their _____ _____ (p. 283).

7. The word _____ is often used to refer to the biological attributes of men and women (p. 280).

8. In comparison with pay equity, which covers wage issues only, _____ _____ deals with recruitment, selection, training, development, and promotion issues (p. 301).

9. The _____ perspective views men and women as having distinct roles that are important for the survival of the family and society (p. 303).

10. According to _____ feminists, male domination causes all forms of human oppression (p. 306).

Matching Items

1. Match the type of society to its key feature.

___ (a) hunting and gathering

___ (b) horticultural
___ (c) agrarian

___ (d) industrialized

1. Women's status decreases with domestication of large animals.
2. Gender equality exists.
3. Purdah and genital mutilation lower women's status.
4. A slender body in females enhances social status.

2. Match the gender socialization agent with its key attribute.

___ (a) parents

___ (b) peers

___ (c) teachers

___ (d) mass media

1. Devotes more time, effort, and attention to boys than girls.
2. Purchase clothing and toys that reflect gender expectations.
3. Are most influential during adolescence.
4. Reinforce the notion that women can never be too young or too thin.

3. Match the theoretical perspective to its key argument.

___ (a) functionalist

___ (b) conflict

___ (c) liberal feminism

___ (d) radical feminism

___ (e) socialist feminism

1. Gender stratification results from private ownership of the means of production.

2. A husband should perform instrumental tasks and a wife, the expressive ones.

3. Women's oppression results from their dual roles as paid and unpaid worker.

4. Gender equality is equated with equality of opportunity.

5. Male domination causes all forms of human oppression.

CHAPTER 10
HEALTH AND HEALTH CARE

Chapter Outline

Health and Medicine
Sociological Perspectives on Health
      Functionalist Perspective on Health: The Sick Role
      Symbolic Interactionist Theory: The Social Construction of Illness
      Conflict Theory: Inequalities in Health and Health Care
Social Factors in Health: Age, Race, Class, and Gender
      Age
      Sex
      Social Class
Disability
      Disability in Historical Perspective
      Disability in Contemporary Society
Social Development and Health: A Global Perspective
      Health Care in Canada
      Universal Health Care
New Approaches to Health Care
      The Medical Model of Illness
      Alternative Approaches
Health Care Issues in the Twenty-First Century

Chapter Summary

Health includes both the absense of disease and a positive sense of wellness. **Medicine** is institutionalized system for the scientific diagnosis, treatment, and prevention of illness. Functionalist perspectives on health highlight the importance of **sick roles**, patterns of behaviour defined as appropriate for people who are sick, and view illness as dysfunctional for both the individual who is sick and for the larger society. In contrast, symbolic interactionists try to understand the social definition of illness and meaning of illness for the individual experiencing health problems. Conflict approaches consider the political and social forces that affect health and the health care system including the ability of all citizens to obtain health care; the impact of race, class, and gender; the relative power of doctors compared with other health workers; the dominance of the medical model of health care; and the role of profit in the health care system. In Canada, **health care** is **universal** and is a provincial responsibility; each province has its own medical insurance plan that meets five requirements including: universality, comprehensiveness, accessibility, portability, and public administration. **Disability** has been defined in many ways including an inability to work, an organically based impairment, or a health condition that stigmatizes or causes discrimination. Disabilties are associated with economic hardship, inadequate government assistance programs, and negative social attitudes toward disabled persons. As we approach the twenty-first century, we can expect continuance in the trend from hospital-based care to home-based care. In addiiton, new reproductive technologies which will continue to create difficult social and ethical dilemmas for Canadians.

Key Terms

health (p. 314)	preventive medicine (p. 314)
health care (p. 314)	senile dementia (p. 322)
medicalization (p. 317)	sick role (p. 314)
medicine (p. 314)	universal health care system (p. 330)

Review of Key Terms

_____ 1. The process whereby an object or a condition becomes defined by society as a physical or psychological illness.

_____ 2. A state of complete physical, mental, and social well-being.

_____ 3. Any activity intended to improve health.

_____ 4. Patterns of behaviour defined as appropriate for people who are sick.

_____ 5. An institutionalized system for the scientific diagnosis, treatment, and prevention of illness.

_____ 6. Medicine that emphasizes a healthy lifestyle in order to prevent poor health before it occurs.

_____ 7. A term for diseases, such as Alzheimer's, that involve a progressive impairment of judgment and memory.

_____ 8. A system in which all citizens receive medical services paid for through taxation revenues.

Key People

Michael Oliver (p. 324)	Ingrid Waldron (p. 322)
Talcott Parsons (p. 314)	Meria Weiss (p. 326)
Peter Conrad and Joseph Schneider (p. 319)	

Review of Key People

_____ 1. A functionalist who claims that all societies have a sick role in which the sick person is exempt for normal social responsibilities.

_____ 2. Identified factors that lead to sex differences in mortality rates.

_____ 3. Found that medicalization is typically the result of a lengthy promotional campaign conducted by interest groups.

_____ 4. Used the term "disability oppression" to describe the barriers that exist for disabled persons in Canadian society.

_____ 5. Challenged the assumption that parents automatically bond with infants, especially those born with visible disabilities.

Learning Objectives

After reading Chapter 10, the student should be able to:

1. define health, health care, medicine, and preventive medicine (p. 314).

2. list and describe the key characteristics of the sick role, as outlined by the functionalist perspective (pp. 314-317).

3. explain how symbolic interactions view health as a social construction of illness (pp. 317-319).

4. describe how the conflict theory view inequalities in health and health care (p. 319).

5. list some of the social factors that influence mortality rates in Canada (pp. 322-323).

6. understand how the term "disability" can be defined in many ways (pp. 324-327).

7. note how Canada ranks globally in terms of its health care system (pp. 329-330).

8. list and describe key requirements of provincial health care plans (pp. 331-332).

9. describe the medical model of illness in Western society (p. 333).

10. list the key trends in health care issues expected for the 21st century (pp. 335-336).

Learning Objective Tests

Multiple Choice Questions

1. Which of the following statements about social factors in health is FALSE?
    a. Males have higher survival rates than females at every stage from fetus to old age.
    b. Rates of illness and death are highest among the old and the young.
    c. Prior to this century, women had lower life expectancies than men due to deaths resulting from pregnancy and childbirth.
    d. The poor have worse health and die earlier than the rich.

2. Disability refers to:
    a. an inability to engage in gainful employment.
    b. an organically based impairment.
    c. a physical or health condition that stigmatizes or causes discrimination.
    d. all of the above are definitions of disability.

3. Any activity that is designed to improve health would be considered:
    a. medicine
    b. health
    c. health care
    d. disease free

4. Which perspective claims that the meaning that social actors give their illness will affect their own self-concept as well as relationships with others?
    a. symbolic interactionist
    b. conflict
    c. functionalist
    d. medical

5. The conflict approach to health care:
    a. emphasizes the meaning a person gives to his or her illness.
    b. considers the inequities that result from political and social forces.
    c. views illness as dysfunctional both for the individual who is sick and for the larger societies.
    d. views the sick role as functional in helping an individual overcome illness.

6. All of the following are key characteristics of the sick role EXCEPT:
    a. The sick person is exempt from normal social responsibilities.
    b. The sick person must want to get well.
    c. The sick person should seek technically competent help and cooperate with health care practitioners.
    d. The sick person must assume responsibility for his or her condition.

7. Which of the following statements about health care in Canada is FALSE?
   a. Prior to the 1906s Canadians had a "user pay" health care system.
   b. In 1997, the United Nations ranked Canada the best place in the world to live.
   c. Health care is a provincial responsibility.
   d. Most Canadians report being "very dissatisfied" with the current Canadian health care program.

8. All of the following are key requirements of provincial health standards EXCEPT:
   a. All Canadians should be coverd on a first come, first served basis.
   b. All necessary medical services should be guaranteed, without dollar limits, and should be available solely on the basis of medical need.
   c. Benefits should be transferable from province to province.
   d. Health care should be operated on a nonprofit basis by a public agency.

9. Which of the following describes a predicted trend in health care for the twenty-first century?
   a. New reproductive technologies will continue to create difficult social and ethical problems.
   b. The evolution from hospital-based care to home-based care will continue.
   c. Unless there is a major shift in the economy, major cuts to health care are unlikely.
   d. all of the above are are predicted trends for the twenty-first century.

10. The medical model assumes that:
    a. illness is deviation from normal.
    b. illness is specific and universal.
    c. illness is caused by biological forces.
    d. all of the above.

True–False Statements

TF 1. Talcott Parsons viewed illness as dysfunctional for both the individual who is sick and for the larger society (p. 314).

TF 2. The social definition of an illness always has a basis in medical fact (p. 317).

TF 3. Rates of illness and death are highest among the old and the young (p. 322).

TF 4. Access to medical care improves the health of the poor (p. 323).

TF 5. Health care is a federal responsibility; and each province has the same medical insurance plan (p. 331).

Fill-in-the-Blanks

1. _____ refers to the process whereby an object or a condition becomes defined by society as a physical or psychological illness (p. 317).

2. Michael Liver (1990) usd the term _____ _____ to describe the barriers that exist for disabled persons in Canadian society (p. 324).

3. A _____ _____ _____ system is one in which all citizens receive medical services paid for through taxation revenues (p. 330).

4. Reasonable access to health care is referred to as _____ (p. 331).

5. _____ is a philosophical principle which encompasses the idea of the whole being greater than the sum of its parts (p. 334).

CHAPTER 11
THE ECONOMY AND WORK

Chapter Outline

Chapter Summary

The **economy** is the social institution that ensures the maintenance of society through the production, distribution, and consumption of goods and services. Preindustrial societies are characterized by **primary sector production,** in which workers extract raw materials and natural resources from the environment. Industrial societies engage in **secondary sector production,** which is based on the processing of raw materials into finished goods. Postindustrial societies involve **tertiary sector production**—the provision of services rather than goods. **Capitalism** includes private ownership of the means of production, pursuit of personal profit, competition, and lack of government intervention. **Socialism** is characterized by public ownership, collective goals, and centralized decision making. **Democratic socialism** is a system that combines private ownership of some of the means of production, governmental distribution of some goods and services, and free elections. **Occupations** are categories of jobs that involve similar activities at different work sites. **Professions** are high-status, knowledge-based occupations characterized by abstract, specialized knowledge, autonomy, and authority over clients. **Marginal jobs** violate employment norms such as adequate hours and pay or government regulation. **Contingent work** is part-time work, temporary work, and subcontracted work. **Unemployment** remains a problem for many workers. As we approach the 21st century, the gap between the rich and the poor is growing.

Key Terms

capitalism (p. 346)
conglomerates (p. 349)
contingent work (p. 357)
corporations (p. 347)
democratic socialism (p. 352)
economy (p. 342)
labour union (p. 360)
marginal jobs (p. 356)
mixed economy (p. 351)
multinational corporations (p. 348)

occupations (p. 354)
oligopoly (p. 349)
primary sector production (p. 344)
professions (p. 355)
secondary sector production (p. 344)
shared monopoly (p. 349)
socialism (p. 350)
tertiary sector production (p. 344)
unemployment rate (p. 358)

Review of Key Terms

_____ 1. The extraction of raw materials and natural resources from the environment.

_____ 2. The processing of raw materials (from the primary sector) into finished goods.

_____ 3. The provision of services rather than goods as the primary source of livelihood for workers and profit for owners and corporate shareholders.

_____ 4. Exists when several companies overwhelmingly control an entire industry.

_____ 5. Exists when four or fewer companies supply 50 percent or more of a particular market.

_____ 6. The social institution that ensures the maintenance of society through the production, distribution, and consumption of goods and services.

_____ 7. Large companies that are headquartered in one country and have subsidiaries or branches in other countries.

_____ 8. Combinations of businesses in different commercial areas, all of which are owned by one holding company.

_____ 9. Are high-status, knowledge-based occupations.

_____ 10. Are categories of jobs that involve similar activities at different work sites.

_____ 11. An economic system characterized by public ownership of the means of production, the pursuit of collective goals, and centralized decision making.

_____ 12. An economic system characterized by private ownership of the means of production, from which personal profits can be derived through market competition and without government intervention.

_____ 13. Large scale organizations that have legal powers, such as the ability to enter into contracts and buy and sell property, separately from their individual owners.

_____ 14. An economic and political system that combines private ownership of some of the means of production, governmental distribution of some essential goods and services, and free elections.

_____ 15. Is the percentage of unemployed persons in the labour force actively seeking jobs.

_____ 16. Combines the elements of a market economy (capitalism) with the elements of a command economy (socialism).

_____ 17. Differ from the employment norms of the society in which they are located.

_____ 18. Part-time work or temporary work.

_____ 19. A group of employees who join together to bargain with an employer or a group of employers over wages, benefits, and working conditions.

Key People

Harold Innis (p. 346)
Harvey Krahn (p. 357)
Kari Levitt (p. 348)

Katherine Marshall (p. 355)
Karl Marx (p. 350)
Adam Smith (p. 349)

Review of Key People

_____ 1. Showed how the early Canadian economy was driven by the demands for raw materials by the colonial powers of France and Britain.

_____ 2. Found that between 1976 and 1994, the number of part-time jobs increased at an average rate of 6.9 percent annually, whereas the rate was 1.5 percent for full-time jobs.

_____ 3. Wrote *The Communist Manifesto* and *Das Kapital*, in which he predicted that the working class would become increasingly impoverished and alienated under capitalism.

_____ 4. Found that women have made significant gains in the professions.

_____ 5. Was among the first to show how this foreign private investment posed a threat to Canadian sovereignty as fundamental economic decisions were made outside the country.

_____ 6. Advocated a policy of laissez-faire in his 1776 treatise, *An Inquiry into the Nature and Causes of the Wealth of Nations.*

Learning Objectives

After reading Chapter 11, the student should be able to:

1. describe the purpose of economy and distinguish between goods, services, labour, and capital (p. 342).

2. trace the major historical changes that have occurred in economic systems and note the most prevalent form of production found in each (pp. 344-346).

3. describe the four distinctive features of "ideal" capitalism and explain why pure capitalism does not exist (pp. 346-350).

4. define and distinguish between corporations and multinational corporations (pp. 347-348).

5. define and distinguish between an oligopoly, shared monopoly, and conglomerate (p. 349).

6. discuss socialism and describe its major characteristics (pp. 350-351).

7. explain how a functionalist perspective views the economy and work (pp. 352-353).

8. describe job satisfaction and alienation and explain the impact of each on workers (p. 354).

9. discuss the major characteristics of professions (pp. 354-355).

10. identify the occupational categories considered to be marginal jobs and explain why they are classified as marginal (pp. 356-357).

11. define contingent work and explain how it benefits employers (pp. 357-358).

12. list and distinguish between the various types of unemployment (pp. 358-360).

13. trace the development of labour unions and describe some of the means by which workers resist working conditions they consider to be oppressive (pp. 360-362).

14. explain why economist and futurist Jeremy Rifkin (1995) thinks that work as we know it is coming to an end (pp. 362-364).

Learning Objective Tests

Multiple Choice Questions

1. Which of the following statements about historical economic systems is TRUE?
   a. Preindustrial economies are based on tertiary-sector production.
   b. Industrial economies are based on secondary-sector production.
   c. Postindustrial economies are based on the extraction of raw materials and natural resources from the environment.
   d. Postindustrial economies are based on the processing of raw materials into finished goods.

2. A(n) _____ exists when four or fewer companies supply 50 percent or more of a particular market:
   a. oligopoly.
   b. shared monopoly.
   c. conglomerate.
   d. corporation.

3. All of the following are key characteristics of professions EXCEPT:
   a. autonomy.
   b. self-regulation.
   c. job segmentation.
   d. authority.

4. In an effort to improve work conditions and gain some measure of control over their own work-related activities, workers:
   a. joined conglomerates.
   b. created an oligopoly.
   c. formed labour unions.
   d. alienated management until demands were met.

5. Which of the following is an essential component of the economy?
   a. goods and services
   b. labour
   c. capital
   d. all of the above make up the economy

6. Job satisfaction refers to people's attitudes toward their work based on:
   a. their job responsibilities.
   b. the organizational structure in which they work.
   c. their individual needs and values.
   d. all of the above.

7. A job is considered marginal if it:
   a. provides adequate pay with sufficient hours to make a living.
   b. is not covered by government work regulations, such as minimum standards of pay.
   c. is permanent.
   d. includes positions in the lower tier of the service sector.

8. According to Jeremy Rifton's analysis:
   a. bank machines will replace tellers.
   b. robots will replace factory workers.
   c. knowledge workers (e.g., engineers) will benefit the most.
   d. all of the above will take place in the 21st century.

9. All of the following are major forms of unemployment EXCEPT:
   a. cyclical.
   b. marginal.
   c. seasonal.
   d. structural.

10. Large-scale organizations that have the legal power to buy and sell property separate from their individual owners are called:
    a. corporations.
    b. mixed economies.
    c. conglomerates.
    d. interlocking corporate directorates.

11. Ideal capitalism contains all of the following characteristics EXCEPT:
    a. private ownership of the means of production.
    b. pursuit of personal profit.
    c. competition.
    d. government intervention.

12. Which perspective views the economy as a vital institution because it is the means by which needed goods and services are provided and distributed?
    a. functionalist
    b. conflict
    c. feminist
    d. interactionist

13. Ideal socialism is based on:
    a. private ownership of the means of production.
    b. pursuit of individual goals.
    c. centralized decision making.
    d. all of the above.

14. Part-time work or temporary employment is referred to as:
    a. marginal work.
    b. contingent work.
    c. personal service work.
    d. cyclical work.

True–False Statements

TF   1. Postindustrial societies are based on secondary-sector production (p. 344).

TF   2. Capitalism involves the pursuit of collective goals (p. 346).

TF   3. In a truly socialist economy, the means of production are owned and controlled by a collectivity (p. 350).

TF   4. From a conflict perspective, business cycles are the result of capitalist greed (p. 353).

TF   5. Positions in the lower tier of the service sector are characterized by low wages, little job security, and few chances for advancement (p. 356).

TF   6. Cyclical employment occurs because the skills demanded by employers do not match the skills of the unemployed (p. 358).

TF   7. Canada's regions have similar rates of unemployment (p. 359).

TF   8. Unemployment rates vary by gender (p. 359).

Fill-in-the-Blanks

1. _____ are intangible activities for which people are willing to pay (e.g., dry cleaning) (p. 342).

2. _____ consists of the physical and intellectual services, including training, education, and individual abilities, that people contribute to the production process (p. 342).

3. _____ is the wealth (money or property) owned or used in business by a person or corporation (p. 342).

4. _____ _____ _____, or the provision of services includes a wide range of activities, including transportation, education, real estate, and entertainment (p. 344).

5. In theory, _____ acts as a balance to excessive profits (p. 348).

6.   Sweden and France have mixed economies, sometimes referred to as _____ _____ (p. 352).

7.   _____ _____ refers to people's attitudes toward their work, based on their job responsibilities, the organizational structure in which they work, and their individual needs and values (p. 354).

Matching Items

1. Match the economy to its key characteristic.

___ (a) preindustrial economy
___ (b) industrial economy
___ (c) postindustrial economy

1. tertiary-service production
2. secondary-sector production
3. primary-sector production

2. Match the economic system with its corresponding feature.

___ (a) capitalism
___ (b) socialism
___ (c) mixed economy

1. public ownership of the means of production
2. private and government ownership
3. private ownership of the means of production

CHAPTER 12
POLITICS AND GOVERNMENT

Chapter Outline

Chapter Summary

The relationship between politics and power is a strong one in all countries. **Politics** is the social institution through which power is acquired and exercised by some people or groups. **Power** is the ability of persons or groups to carry out their will even in the face of opposition. Most leaders seek to legitimate their power through **authority**—power that people accept as legitimate rather than coercive. According to Max Weber, there are three types of authority: (1) charismatic, (2) traditional, and (3) rational–legal (bureaucratic). There are four main types of contemporary political systems: monarchy, authoritarianism, totalitarianism, and democracy. In a **democracy** the people hold the ruling power, either directly or through elected representatives. According to the **pluralist model,** power in democratic governments is widely dispersed throughout many competing interest groups. According to the **elite model,** power is concentrated among the elite and the masses are relatively powerless. The **power elite** comprises of influential business leaders, key government leaders, and the military. **Political parties** are organizations whose purpose is to gain and hold legitimate control of government. The Liberals and the Progressive Conservatives have dominated the Canadian political system since Confederation. People learn political attitudes, values, and behaviours through **political socialization.** The vast governmental bureaucracy is a major source of power. Transnational trends have made it increasingly difficult for all forms of governments to control events. While these trends will become more complex in the 21st century, people are still likely to depend on their governments to lead and to provide solutions.

Key Terms

authoritarianism (p. 378)

authority (p. 374)

charismatic authority (p. 374)

democracy (p. 379)

elite model (p. 381)

government (p. 374)

monarchy (p. 378)

pluralist model (p. 380)

political party (p. 383)

political socialization (p. 384)

politics (p. 374)

power (p. 374)

power elite (p. 382)

rational–legal authority (p. 376)

routinization of charisma (p. 374)

special interest groups (p. 380)

state (p. 374)

totalitarianism (p. 378)

traditional authority (p. 375)

Review of Key Terms

_____ 1. The social institution through which power is acquired and exercised by some people and groups.

_____ 2. The political entity that possesses a legitimate monopoly over the use of force within its territory to achieve its goals.

_____ 3. Power that is legitimized by respect for long-standing custom.

_____ 4. The formal organization that has the legal and political authority to regulate the relationships among members of a society and between the society and those outside its borders.

_____ 5. Power legitimized by law or written rules and regulations.

_____ 6. A political system in which power resides in one person or family and is passed from generation to generation through lines of inheritance.

_____ 7. Composed of leaders at the top of business, the executive branch of the federal government, and the military.

_____ 8. An organization whose purpose is to gain and hold legitimate control of government.

_____ 9. The ability of persons or groups to carry out their will even when opposed by others.

_____ 10. Occurs when charismatic authority is succeeded by a bureaucracy controlled by a rationally established authority or by a combination of traditional and bureaucratic authority.

_____ 11. Power that people accept as legitimate rather than coercive.

_____ 12. According to this model, power is widely dispersed throughout many competing interest groups.

_____ 13. Power legitimized on the basis of a leader's exceptional personal qualities.

_____ 14. Political coalitions made up of individuals or groups that share a specific interest they wish to protect or advance with the help of the political system.

_____ 15. A political system controlled by rulers who deny popular participation in government.

_____ 16. A political system in which the state seeks to regulate all aspects of people's public and private lives.

_____ 17. A political system in which the people hold the ruling power directly or through elected representatives.

_____ 18. According to this model, power in political systems is concentrated in the hands of a small group of elites and the masses are relatively powerless.

_____ 19. The process by which people learn political attitudes, values, and behaviour.

Key People

Menno Boldt (p. 391)
Ramsay Cook (p. 393)
Olive Dickason (p. 389)
G. William Domhoff (p. 383)
Emile Durkheim (p. 380)

Thomas R. Dye and
    Harmon Zeigler (p. 381)
C. Wright Mills (p. 382)
Pierre Vallières (p. 370)
Max Weber (p. 374)

Review of Key People

_____ 1. Pointed out that when the Europeans first came to North America, 55 aboriginal First Nations were on the continent.

_____ 2. Used the term *ruling class* to signify a relatively fixed group of privileged people who wield sufficient power to constrain political processes and serve underlying capitalist interests.

_____ 3. Summarized the key elements of pluralism.

_____ 4. Claimed that the purpose of government is to socialize people to become good citizens, to regulate the economy so that it operates effectively, and to provide the necessary services for citizens.

_____ 5. Claimed that the powerlessness of Indians is the result of Canada's Indian policies.

_____ 6. Examined the role of nationalism in justifying one's place in the world.

_____ 7. Examined the power structure of the United States and speculated that the corporate rich were the most powerful.

_____ 8. Claimed that a charismatic leader could be either a tyrant or a hero.

_____ 9. Was one of the intellectual leaders of the FLQ (the Front de Libération du Québec).

Learning Objectives

After reading Chapter 12, the student should be able to:

1. explain the relationship between politics, government, and the state (p. 374).

2. distinguish between power and authority (p. 374).

3. define and describe what is meant by charismatic authority (pp. 374-375).

4. define and describe what is meant by traditional authority (p. 375).

5. define and describe what is meant by rational–legal authority (pp. 376-377).

6. describe the key features of governments characterized by monarchy, authoritarianism, and totalitarianism (pp. 378-379).

7. describe the key features of governments characterized by democracy (p. 379).

8. state the major elements of the pluralist (functionalist) model of power and political systems (pp. 380-381).

9. state the major elements of elite (conflict) models of power and political systems (pp. 381-383)

10. define political party and analyze how well Canadian parties measure up to the ideal-type characteristics of political parties (pp. 384-384).

11. explain the relationship between political socialization, political attitudes, and political participation (pp. 384-387).

12. discuss some of the causes and consequences of Quebec nationalism (pp. 388-389).

13. describe the case made by the aboriginal people for self-government (p. 389-392).

Learning Objective Tests

Multiple Choice Questions

1. According to Weber, _____ is power that is legitimized through formal rules and laws.
   a. rational–legal authority
   b. charismatic authority
   c. traditional authority
   d. exceptional authority

2. All of the following are key elements of pluralism EXCEPT:
   a. Decisions are made on behalf of the people by leaders who engage in a process of bargaining.
   b. Competition among leadership groups makes abuse of power more difficult.
   c. People can influence public policy by voting in elections.
   d. Power is very narrowly dispersed and public policy is always based on majority preference.

3. Which of the following statements best illustrates the relationship between politics and government?
   a. Politics involve government, but government does not involve politics.
   b. Politics is the ability of people to carry out their will, while government carries out orders regardless of people's will.
   c. In contemporary societies, the government is the primary political system.
   d. All of the above illustrate the relationship between politics and government.

4. Traditional authority involves:
   a. charismatic leadership.
   b. respect for custom.
   c. legitimation through laws.
   d. all of the above.

5. Which of the following statements describes how Canadian political parties measure up to the ideal-type characteristics presented in Chapter 12?
   a. The two major parties rarely offer voters clear policy alternatives.
   b. Most political parties are dominated by active elites who are not representative of the general population.
   c. The electoral system in Canada effectively limits the degree to which a diversity of views is reflected in our legislatures.
   d. All of the above are problems with Canadian political parties.

6. Totalitarianism is a political system in which:
    a. the state seeks to regulate all aspects of people's lives.
    b. rulers deny popular participation in government.
    c. the people hold the ruling power.
    d. citizens elect representatives to serve as bridges between themselves and the government.

7. Political participation includes:
    a. voting.
    b. attending and taking part in political meetings.
    c. running for, or holding, political office.
    d. all of the above demonstrate political participation.

8. According to Weber, charismatic authority is characterized by:
    a. respect for long-standing custom.
    b. legitimation through laws, rules, and regulations.
    c. a leader's exceptional personal qualities.
    d. none of the above.

9. The literal meaning of democracy is:
    a. thinking and behaving for oneself.
    b. rule by the people.
    c. absolute monarchy.
    d. military dictatorship.

10. The key factor promoting Quebec nationalism is:
    a. hatred for English Canadians.
    b. a desire for unilingualism.
    c. extreme Quebec nationalism.
    d. a feeling of alienation.

11. Which of the following statements about power and authority is TRUE?
    a. Power is when people accept things as legitimate because of charisma.
    b. People have a greater tendency to accept authority as legitimate if they are economically or politically dependent on those who hold power.
    c. The most basic form of authority is force or military action.
    d. Power and authority cannot exist at the same time.

12. All of the following are major elements of elite (conflict) models of power EXCEPT:
    a. The masses have little influence over the elite and public policy.
    b. Individual rights are protected.
    c. Power is highly concentrated at the top of a pyramid-shaped social hierarchy; those at the top come together to set policy for everyone.
    d. Consensus exists among the elite as to the basic goals and values of society.

13. Which statement concerning aboriginal people in Canada is FALSE?
    a. Fifty-five aboriginal First Nations were on the continent when Europeans first came to North America.
    b. Following Confederation, aboriginal people came under the control of the government.
    c. Native people maintained full voting rights in federal elections from 1876 to present.
    d. As a consequence of the Indian Act, aboriginal children were forced to attend residential schools.

True–False Statements

TF 1. Traditional authority tends to be temporary and unstable; it derives primarily from individual leaders and from an administrative structure (p. 374).

TF 2. Functionalist perspectives assume that government exists for the benefit of wealthy or politically powerful elites who use the government to impose their will on the masses (p. 380).

TF 3. There is a very high association between social class and voting behaviour (p. 386).

TF 4. Quebec separatism and Aboriginal self-government continue to be major political issues in Canada (pp. 388-392).

TF 5. Aboriginal people feel their status as Canada's first people entitles them to the right of self-determination and to protection of their culture and customs (p. 391).

Fill-in-the-Blanks

1. In contemporary society, the _____ is the primary political system (p. 374).

2. Through the use of _____, people's actions are channeled in one direction rather than another on the assumption that meeting some collective goal is more important than satisfying individual needs and wants (p. 374).

3. _____ refers to the process by which power is institutionalized and given a moral foundation to justify its existence (p. 374).

4. To Weber, _____ individuals have exceptional personal qualities or demonstrate extraordinary insight which inspires loyalty and obedience from followers (p. 374).

5. With _____ - _____ _____, the authority is invested in the office, not in the person who holds the office (p. 376).

6. The _____ of _____ and _____, which is entrenched in the Canadian Constitution, guarantees that all Canadians have the right to democratic participation (p. 379).

7. _____ relies on modern technology to monitor and control people; mass propaganda and electronic surveillance are widely used to influence peoples' thinking and control their actions (p. 378).

8. Those with a _____ perspective on social issues tend to believe that women have the right to an abortion, that criminals should be rehabilitated, and that the government has an obligation to protect the rights of subordinate groups (p. 385).

Matching Items

1. Match the political system with it main characteristic.

___ (a) monarchy

___ (b) authoritarianism

___ (c) totalitarianism

___ (d) democracy

1. state regulation

2. ruled by the people

3. power in one family

4. denies popular participation

2. Match the type of authority with its key feature.

___ (a) charismatic authority

___ (b) traditional authority

___ (c) rational-legal authority

1. exceptional personal qualities

2. written rules and regulations

3. respect for custom

CHAPTER 13
FAMILIES AND INTIMATE RELATIONSHIPS

Chapter Outline

Chapter Summary

Families are relationships in which people live together with commitment, form an economic unit and care for any young. While the **family of orientation** is the family into which a person is born and in which early socialization usually takes place, the **family of procreation** is the family a person forms by having or adopting children. Sociologists investigate marriage patterns (i.e., **monogamy** and **polygamy**), descent and inheritance patterns (i.e., **patrilineal, matrilineal,** and **bilateral** descent), familial power and authority (i.e., **patriarchal, matriarchal,** and **egalitarian** families), residential patterns (i.e., **patrilocal, matrilocal,** and **neolocal** residence), and in-group or out-group marriage patterns (i.e., **endogamy** and **exogamy**). Functionalists emphasize that families fulfill important societal functions, including sexual regulation, socialization of children, economic and psychological support, and the provision of social status. By contrast, conflict and feminist perspectives view the family as a source of social inequality and focus primarily on the problems inherent in relationships of dominance and subordination. Interactionists focus on family communication patterns and subjective meanings that members assign to everyday events. Families have changed dramatically in Canada; there have been significant increases in cohabitation, domestic partnerships, dual-earner marriages, single-parent families, and rates of divorce and remarriage. Divorce has contributed to greater diversity in family relationships, including stepfamilies or blended families and the complex binuclear family. While some never-married singles choose to remain single, others do so out of necessity.

Key Terms

bilateral descent (p. 403)
cohabitation (p. 414)
domestic partnerships (p. 415)
dual-earner marriages (p. 416)
egalitarian family (p. 406)
endogamy (p. 406)
exogamy (p. 406)
extended family (p. 403)
families (p. 401)
family of orientation (p. 403)
family of procreation (p. 403)
homogamy (p. 416)
kinship (p. 402)
marriage (p. 405)

matriarchal family (p. 406)
matrilineal descent (p. 405)
matrilocal residence (p. 406)
monogamy (p. 405)
neolocal residence (p. 406)
nuclear family (p. 403)
patriarchal family (p. 406)
patrilineal descent (p. 405)
patrilocal residence (p. 518)
polyandry (p. 405)
polygamy (p. 405)
polygyny (p. 405)
second shift (p. 416)
sociology of family (p. 407)

Review of Key Terms

_____ 1. Refers to a situation where a couple live together without being legally married.

_____ 2. A marriage between two partners of the opposite sex.

_____ 3. A family composed of one or two parents and their dependent children, all of whom live apart from other relatives.

_____ 4. Cultural norms prescribing that people marry within their own social group or category.

_____ 5. A family structure in which authority is held by the eldest female.

_____ 6. A family structure in which authority is held by the eldest male.

_____ 7. A system of tracing descent through the mother's side of the family.

_____ 8. A system of tracing descent through the father's side of the family.

_____ 9. The custom of a married couple living in the same household as the wife's parents.

_____ 10. The custom of a married couple living in the same household as the husband's parents.

_____ 11. The family into which a person is born and in which early socialization usually takes place.

_____ 12. The family a person forms by having or adopting children.

_____ 13. The concurrent marriage of a person of one sex with two or more members of the opposite sex.

_____ 14. Marriage of one woman with two or more men.

_____ 15. The concurrent marriage of one man with two or more women.

_____ 16. The domestic work that employed women perform at home after they complete their workday on the job.

_____ 17. Relationships in which people live together with commitment, form an economic unit, care for the young, and consider their identity to be significantly attached to the group.

_____ 18. A system of tracing descent through both the mother's and father's sides of the family.

_____ 19. Household partnerships in which an unmarried couple lives together in a committed, sexually intimate relationship and is granted the same rights and benefits as those accorded married heterosexual couples.

_____ 20. Marriages in which both spouses are in the labour force.

_____ 21. A family structure in which both partners share power and authority equally.

_____ 22. Refers to cultural norms prescribing that people marry outside their own social group or category.

_____ 23. A family unit composed of relatives in addition to parents and children who all live in the same household.

_____ 24. The subdiscipline of sociology that attempts to describe and explain patterns of family life and variations in family structure.

_____ 25. The custom of a married couple living in their own residence apart from both the husband's and wife's parents.

_____ 26. The pattern of individuals marrying those who have similar characteristics, such as race/ethnicity, religious background, and age.

_____ 27. A legally recognized and/or socially approved arrangement between two or more individuals that carries certain rights and obligations and usually involves sexual activity.

_____ 28. Refers to a social network of people based on common ancestry, marriage, or adoption.

Key People

Peter Berger and
   Hansfried Kellner (p. 410)
Jessie Bernard (p. 410)
Emile Durkheim (p. 407)
Arlie Hochschild (p. 416)
Holly Johnson (p. 411)

Meg Luxton (p. 408)
Charlene Maill (p. 418)
Sara McLanahan and Karen Booth (p. 420)
Talcott Parsons (p. 407)
Alice Rossi (p. 421)

Review of Key People

_____ 1. Argued from a functionalist view that marriage is a replica of the larger society.

_____ 2. Claimed that interaction between marital partners contributes to a shared reality.

_____ 3. Outlined the instrumental and expressive roles of husbands and wives.

_____ 4. Argued that women and men experience marriage differently.

_____ 5. Highlighted the dependency created in patriarchal family systems.

_____ 6. Contended that maternity is the mark of adulthood for women, whether or not they are employed.

_____ 7. Explained how involuntarily childless women engage in "information management" to combat social stigma.

_____ 8. Examined the criminal justice system's response to domestic abuse.

_____ 9. Claimed that children in mother-only families are more likely than children in two-parent families to have poor academic achievement, higher divorce rates, and more involvement in alcohol and drugs.

_____ 10. Coined the term "second shift" to describe the domestic work that employed women perform at home.

Learning Objectives

After reading Chapter 13, the student should be able to:

1. explain why it has become increasingly difficult to develop a concise definition of family (pp. 400-401).

2. describe kinship ties and explain how social institutions fulfill the role of kinship (pp. 402-403).

3. distinguish between families of orientation and families of procreation (p. 403).

4. compare and contrast extended and nuclear families (pp. 403-405).

5. define marriage and indicate what forms are legally sanctioned in Canada (p. 405).

6. describe the different forms of marriage found across cultures (p. 405).

7. discuss the system of descent and inheritance, and explain why such systems are important in societies (p. 405).

8. distinguish between patriarchal, matriarchal, and egalitarian families (p. 406).

9. explain the differences between patrilocal and matrilocal residential patterns (p. 406).

10. distinguish between endogamy and exogamy and indicate why most people practice endogamy (p. 406).

11. outline the key functions served by families in advanced industrial societies (pp. 407-408).

12. describe how the conflict and feminist perspectives view families (p. 408).

13. outline the key assumptions of interactionist perspectives on the family (pp. 408-410).

14. describe how Canadian families and intimate relationships have changed over the past two decades (pp. 412-413).

15. describe cohabitation and domestic partnerships and note key social and legal issues associated with each (pp. 414-416).

16. describe the major problems faced in dual-earner marriages, and note why the double shift most often is a problem for women (pp. 416-417).

17. discuss the major issues associated with adoption, new reproductive technologies, single-parent households, and two-parent households (pp. 418-421).

18. explain the major causes and consequences of divorce and remarriage in Canada (pp. 423-425).

Learning Objective Tests

Multiple Choice Questions

1. The marriage of one woman with two or more men at the same time is called:
    a. monogamy.
    b. polyandry.
    c. polygyny.
    d. serial monogamy.

2. In preindustrial societies, the primary form of social organization was:
    a. neighbourhoods.
    b. kinship ties.
    c. religious ties.
    d. conventional beliefs.

3.   In which residential pattern does the married couple live in their own residence apart from both the husband's and wife's parents?
    a.   patrilocal
    b.   matrilocal
    c.   neolocal
    d.   bilateral

4.   Which of the following statements is an accurate representation of changes in Canada in the past two decades?
    a.   Canadians are marrying at younger ages.
    b.   The proportion of lone-parent families is decreasing.
    c.   Between 1981 and 1995, the number of common-law families decreased by 50 percent.
    d.   Many Canadians are now marrying more than once.

5.   Which of the following statements about conflict and feminist perspectives is FALSE?
    a.   Families are sources of social inequality.
    b.   The exploitation of the lower classes by the upper classes contributes to family problems such as high rates of divorce.
    c.   Families are responsible for providing economic and psychological support to members.
    d.   Feminist perspectives on inequality in families focus on patriarchy rather than class differences.

6.   Which of the following statements about cohabitation is FALSE?
    a.   The proportion of people in common-law unions varies consistently by province.
    b.   Those most likely to cohabit are young adults between the ages of 15 and 24.
    c.   The number of cohabiting couples is decreasing in Canada.
    d.   In Canada and the United States, many lesbian and gay couples cohabit because they cannot enter into legally recognized marital relationships.

7.   Which of the following statements about single-parent households is TRUE?
    a.   In recent years, the number of single-parent households has decreased significantly.
    b.   Most single-parent households are headed by males.
    c.   Gay men cannot be fathers.
    d.   Children in mother-only families are more likely than children in two-parent families to have poor academic achievement.

8. Marriage includes all of the following EXCEPT:
   a. legal recognition.
   b. a socially approved arrangement between two or more individuals.
   c. partnership between members of the same sex.
   d. sexual activity.

9. This kind of family often includes grandparents, uncles, or other relatives who live in close proximity to the parents and children, making it possible to share resources.
   a. network
   b. nuclear
   c. extended
   d. patriarchal

10. In what kind of family structure does the eldest female have authority?
    a. patriarchal
    b. matriarchal
    c. egalitarian
    d. bilateral

11. All of the following are major causes of divorce EXCEPT:
    a. marriage at an early age.
    b. limited economic resources and low wages.
    c. previous marriages.
    d. All of the above are major causes of divorce.

12. In Canada most people practise _____, where they marry people who come from the same social class, racial–ethnic group, and religion.
    a. endogamy
    b. exogamy
    c. polygamy
    d. polygyny

13. In which pattern of descent is inheritance traced through the father's side of the family?
    a. patrilineal
    b. matrilineal
    c. bilateral
    d. unilateral

14. Interactionists explain family relationships in terms of:
    a. men's domination over women.
    b. sources of social inequality and exploitation.
    c. the subjective meanings and everyday interpretations people give to their lives.
    d. functions performed at a macrolevel.

15. All of the following are key functions of the family EXCEPT:
    a. sexual regulation.
    b. socialization.
    c. economic and psychological support.
    d. all of the above are key functions of the family.

16. The family of _____ is the family into which a person is born and in which early socialization usually takes place.
    a. orientation
    b. procreation
    c. extension
    d. descent

17. Today's families do not fit the standard sociological definition due to the prevalence of:
    a. single-parent households.
    b. lesbian and gay couples.
    c. multiple-generation families.
    d. all of the above.

18. Which of the following statements about dual-earner marriages is TRUE?
    a. Women and men perform similar household tasks.
    b. Most employed women work part-time.
    c. The number of cohabiting couples is decreasing in Canada.
    d. In Canada and the United States, many lesbian and gay couples cohabit because they cannot enter into legally recognized marital relationships.

True–False Statements

TF   1.   Most Canadian marriages end in divorce (p. 398).

TF   2.   The average age at marriage is decreasing in Canada (p. 401).

TF   3.   Married couples with children make up the largest category in the family structure of Canadians (p. 404).

TF   4.   The family of procreation is the one into which a person is born and in which early socialization takes place (p. 403).

TF   5.   Patrilineal descent is a system of tracing descent through the mother's side of the family (p. 405).

TF   6.   The number of lone-parent families is on the rise (p. 416).

TF   7.   The most likely to cohabit are young adults between the ages of 15 and 24 (p. 414).

TF   8.   Approximately 62 percent of all marriages in Canada are dual-earner marriages (p. 416).

TF   9.   Most employed women in Canada have full-time, year-round jobs (p. 416).

TF   10. In Canada, adoption is regulated provincially (p. 418).

Fill-in-the-Blanks

1.   The _____ of _____ is the family a person forms by having or adopting children (p. 403).

2.   A traditional definition specifies that a _____ family is made up of a "couple" and their dependent children (p. 403).

3.   In Canada, the only legally sanctioned form of marriage is _____ (p. 405).

4.   The most prevalent form of polygamy is _____, the marriage of one man to more than one woman (p. 405).

5.   The _____ of _____ is the subdiscipline of sociology that attempts to describe and explain patterns of family life (p. 407).

6.   _____ families consist of a husband, wife, children from previous marriages, and children from the new marriage (p. 425).

Matching Items

1. Match the marriage pattern to its defining feature.

____ (a) monogamy   1. two partners of opposite sexes
____ (b) polygyny   2. one wife, two husbands
____ (c) polyandry   3. one husband, two wives

2. Match the residential pattern to its key characteristic.

____ (a) partilocal residence   1. newlyweds live in their own residence
____ (b) matrilocal residence   2. newlyweds live with the wife's family
____ (c) neolocal residence   3. newlyweds live with the husband's family

CHAPTER 14
EDUCATION AND RELIGION

Chapter Outline

Chapter Summary

Education is the social institution responsible for the systematic transmission of knowledge, skills, and cultural values within a formally organized structure. Functionalists focus on how education contributes to socialization, transmission of culture, social control, social placement, and innovation, while conflict theorists emphasize how education perpetuates class, racial–ethnic, and gender inequalities. Interactionists point out that education may be a self-fulfilling prophecy for students who perform in accordance with teacher expectations. **Religion** is a system of beliefs, symbols, and rituals based on some sacred realm that guides human behaviour, gives meaning to life, and unites believers. Advances in scientific knowledge have contributed to **secularization**—the process by which religious beliefs, practices, and institutions lose their significance in society. According to functionalists, religion provides meaning to life, promotes social cohesion, and contributes to social control. From a conflict perspective, the capitalist class uses religion as a tool of domination to mislead workers about their true interests. Interactionists examine the meanings that people give to religion and religious symbols in their everyday life. Contemporary religious organizations include **ecclesia, churches, denominations, sects,** and **cults.** Maintaining an appropriate balance between the social institutions of education and religion will be an important challenge for Canada in the 21st century.

Key Terms

church (p. 452)
cult (p. 453)
cultural capital (p. 439)
denomination (p. 452)
ecclesia (p. 452)
education (p. 436)
hidden curriculum (p. 440)
latent functions (p. 438)

manifest functions (p. 437)
profane (p. 446)
religion (p. 446)
rituals (p. 446)
sacred (p. 446)
sect (p. 453)
self-fulfilling prophecy (p. 441)
tracking (p. 439)

Review of Key Terms

_____ 1. The social institution responsible for the systematic transmission of knowledge, skills, and cultural values within a formally organized structure.

_____ 2. A religious group with practices and teachings outside the dominant cultural and religious traditions of a society.

_____ 3. Open, stated, and intended goals or consequences of activities within an organization or institution.

_____ 4. Hidden, unstated, and sometimes unintended consequences of activities within an organization or institution.

_____ 5. The transmission of cultural values and attitudes, such as conformity and obedience to authority, through implied demands found in rules, routines, and regulations of schools.

_____ 6. An unsubstantiated belief or prediction resulting in behaviour that makes the originally false belief come true.

_____ 7. A system of beliefs, symbols, and rituals, based on some sacred or supernatural realm, that guides human behaviour, gives meaning to life, and unites believers into a community.

_____ 8. Social assets that include values, beliefs, attitudes, and competencies in language and culture.

_____ 9. The categorical assignment of students based on test scores, previous grades, or both, to different types of educational programs.

_____ 10. Refers to those aspects of life that are extraordinary or supernatural.

_____ 11. The everyday, secular, or "worldly" aspects of life.

_____ 12. Symbolic actions that represent religious meanings.

_____ 13. A relatively small religious group that has broken away from another religious organization to renew what it views as the original version of the faith.

_____ 14. A religious organization that is so integrated into the dominant culture that it claims as its membership all members of a society.

_____ 15. A large, bureaucratically organized religious body that tends to seek accommodation with the larger society in order to maintain some degree of control over it.

_____ 16. A large, organized religious body characterized by accommodation to society but frequently lacking the ability or intention to dominate society.

Key People

Reginald Bibby (p. 454)
Pierre Bourdieu (p. 439)
Emile Durkheim (pp. 436; 447)
Clifford Geertz (p. 446)
Karl Marx (p. 450)

Meredith B. McGuire (p. 447)
Robert Merton (p. 441)
Stephen Richer (p. 440)
Robert Rosenthal (p. 442)
Max Weber (p. 450)

Review of Key People

_____ 1. Argued that religious ideologies serve to justify the status quo and retard social change.

_____ 2. A sociologist who claimed that religion was a powerful, deeply felt social institution that played a key role in helping people find meaning and purpose.

_____ 3. Coined the term _self-fulfilling prophecy._

_____ 4. Used a functionalist perspective to argue the fundamental importance of education and religion in society.

_____ 5. An anthropologist who claimed that religion is a set of cultural symbols that establish powerful and pervasive moods and motivations to help people interpret the meaning of life and establish a direction for their behaviour.

_____ 6. Suggested that the hidden curriculum favours students from middle- and upper-class backgrounds.

_____ 7. Designed an experiment to examine the effects of teacher expectations on student performance.

_____ 8. Claimed that Canadians practise "specialized consumption," looking to churches for rites-of-passage ceremonies such as marriage.

_____ 9. Believed that religion served as a catalyst for change.

_____ 10. Coined the term _culture capital._

Learning Objectives

After reading Chapter 14, the student should be able to:

1. describe how a functionalist perspective views education and be able to list the five key manifest functions of education (pp. 436-438).

2. understand how latent functions differ from manifest ones and be able to identify the three key latent functions of education (pp. 438-439).

3. be able to distinguish between functionalist and conflict perspectives on education (pp. 436-441).

4. describe the conflict perspective's view of education as a vehicle for reproducing existing class relationships (pp. 439-441).

5. explain how the conflict perspective defines the "hidden curriculum" and note the implications of the hidden curriculum for social class, credentialism, and gender (pp. 440-441).

6. discuss interactionist perspectives on education and describe the significance of the self-fulfilling prophecy and labelling on educational achievement (pp. 441-444).

7. list and describe current concerns regarding the provincial public education systems (pp. 444-446).

8. describe the functionalist perspective on religion and discuss its major functions in societies (pp. 447-450).

9. compare and contrast Karl Marx and Max Weber's conflict perspectives on religion (pp. 450-451).

10. discuss interactionist perspectives on religion and explain how religion may be viewed differently by women and men (pp. 451-452).

11. distinguish between major religious organizations (e.g., ecclesia, churches, sects, and cults) (pp. 452-454).

12. list the key characteristics of churches and sects identified by Troeltsch and Weber's church-sect typology (pp. 452-453).

13. note whether religiosity is thriving or declining in Canada according to recent trends (pp. 454-457).

Learning Objective Tests

Multiple Choice Questions

1. From a functionalist perspective, religion:
   a. offers meaning for the human experience.
   b. helps promote social cohesion and a sense of belonging.
   c. helps bind society together and maintain social control.
   d. performs all of the functions listed above.

2. Which of the following is a LATENT function of education?
   a. restricting some activities
   b. matchmaking and production of social networks
   c. creation of a generation gap
   d. All of the above are latent functions of education.

3. A religious organization that is so integrated into the dominant culture that it claims as its membership all members of a society is:
   a. the ecclesia.
   b. the church.
   c. a sect.
   d. a cult.

4. All of the following are key characteristics of churches EXCEPT:
   a. intolerant, closely guarded membership.
   b. formal, orderly type of worship.
   c. salvation granted by God.
   d. large bureaucratic organizations.

5. Which perspective argues that schools perpetuate class, racial–ethnic, and gender inequalities in society?
   a. functionalist
   b. conflict
   c. interactionist
   d. realist

6. All of the following represent current issues in Canadian education EXCEPT:
   a. Inadequate standards due to a child-centred system.
   b. A high rate of functional illiteracy.
   c. A high rate of cheating on final examinations.
   d. A high rate of school dropouts.

7. Which of the following factors contributes to the reproduction of class?
    a. Middle- and upper-class parents endow their children with high cultural capital, resulting in higher chances of success in school.
    b. Many Canadian schools practise streaming or tracking of children in various courses and programs.
    c. Student records, test scores, dress, appearance, parental background, sex, and ethnicity combine in a very complex way to affect teacher expectations and evaluations.
    d. All of the above contribute to the reproduction of class.

8. Which of the following statements represents an interactionist view of religion?
    a. For many people, religion serves as a reference group to help them define themselves.
    b. Religion unites people under a "false consciousness" to which they believe they have common interests with members of the dominant class.
    c. Religion helps maintain social control by conferring supernatural legitimacy on the norms and laws in society.
    d. Religion tends to promote conflict between groups and societies.

9. An unsubstantiated belief or prediction resulting in behaviour that makes the originally false belief come true is known as:
    a. a self-fulfilling prophecy.
    b. a negative label.
    c. credentialism.
    d. the hidden curriculum.

10. According to the conflict perspective on religion, which of the following statements is TRUE?
    a. Religion serves positive functions in society.
    b. For Max Weber, religion was viewed as a catalyst for change.
    c. Religion promotes social cohesiveness and a sense of belonging.
    d. All of the above statements are true.

11. Which of the following statements about the "hidden curriculum" is FALSE?
    a. Students from all social classes are subjected to the hidden curriculum.
    b. Middle- and upper-class students may be most adversely affected by the hidden curriculum.
    c. The hidden curriculum in the early grades encourages students to be competitive, materialistic, to value work over play, and to show deference to authority.
    d. Students from lower-class backgrounds are less motivated when rewards for effort are symbolic rather than material.

12. According to Canadian trends concerning religiosity:
    a. church attendance has gradually declined since the late 1940s.
    b. church influence has gradually declined since the 1940s.
    c. many people are becoming involved in new forms of spirituality.
    d. all of the above characterize current trends in religiosity.

13. All of the following are manifest functions of formal education EXCEPT:
    a. socialization.
    b. transmission of culture.
    c. matchmaking and production of social networks.
    d. change and innovation.

True–False Statements

TF 1. Functionalists suggest that education contributes to the maintenance of society and provides people with an opportunity for self-enhancement and upward social mobility (p. 436).

TF 2. An example of a manifest function of education is the creation of a generation gap (pp. 437-438).

TF 3. Although students from all social classes are subjected to the hidden curriculum, working-class and poverty-level students may be most adversely affected (p. 440).

TF 4. Interactionists typically emphasize the ways in which religious beliefs and rituals can bind people together (p. 441).

TF 5. Karl Marx believed that people become complacent because they have been taught to believe in an afterlife in which they are rewarded for their suffering and misery in this life (p. 450).

TF 6. Church membership largely is based on birth; children of church members typically are baptized as infants and become lifelong members of the church (p. 452).

Fill-in-the-Blanks

1. _____ _____ involves the "proper" attitudes toward education, socially approved dress and manners, and knowledge about books, art, music, and other forms of high and popular culture (p. 439).

2. The _____ _____ has been used to explain why so few women study mathematics and science at the postsecondary level (pp. 440-441).

3.   People often act out their religious beliefs in the form of _____, symbolic actions that represent religious meanings (p. 446).

4.   Membership in an _____ occurs as a result of being born into a society, rather than any conscious decision on the part of individual members (p. 452).

5.   Midway between a church and a sect is a _____, a large, organized religious body characterized by accommodation to society but frequently lacking the ability or intention to dominate society (p. 452).

Matching Items

1. Match the concept with the appropriate theoretical perspective on education.

___ (a) social placement   1. functionalist perspective
___ (b) cultural capital   2. conflict perspective
___ (c) self-fulfilling prophecy   3. interactionist perspective

CHAPTER 15
POPULATION AND URBANIZATION

Chapter Outline

Chapter Summary

Demography is the study of the size, composition, and distribution of the population. Population growth results of **fertility** (births), **mortality** (deaths), and **migration.** Over 200 years ago, Thomas Malthus warned that overpopulation would result in global poverty and starvation. According to the Marxist perspective, overpopulation occurs because of capitalist demands for a surplus of workers to suppress wages and heighten workers' productivity. **Demographic transition** is the process by which some societies have moved from high birth and death rates to relatively low ones as a result of technological development. **Urban sociology** is the study of social relationships and political and economic structures in the city. Functionalist perspectives (ecological models) of urban growth include the concentric zone model, the sector model, and the multiple-nuclei model. According to the political economy models of conflict theorists, urban growth is influenced by capital investment decisions, power and resource inequality, class and class conflict, and government subsidy programs. Feminist theorists suggest that cities have gender regimes; women's lives are affected by both public and private patriarchy. Interactionists focus on the positive and negative aspects of people's experiences in the urban settings. Urbanization, suburbanization, gentrification, and the growth of edge cities have had a dramatic impact on the population. Many central cities have experienced fiscal crises that have resulted in cuts in services, lack of maintenance of the infrastructure, and a health care crisis. Rapid global population growth is inevitable in the 21st century.

Key Terms

central city (p. 483)
crude birth rate (p. 466)
crude death rate (p. 466)
demographic transition (p. 480)
demography (p. 463)
emigration (p. 468)
fertility (p. 464)
immigration (p. 468)
infant mortality rate (p. 467)
invasion (p. 485)

life expectancy (p. 468)
megalopolis (p. 492)
metropolis (p. 483)
migration (p. 468)
mortality (p. 466)
population composition (p. 471)
population pyramid (p. 472)
succession (p. 485)
urban sociology (p. 481)

Review of Key Terms

_____ 1. The subfield of sociology that examines population size, composition, and distribution.

_____ 2. A continuous concentration of two or more cities and their suburbs that have grown until they form an interconnected urban area.

_____ 3. The actual level of childbearing for an individual or a population.

_____ 4. The process by which some societies have moved from high birth and death rates to relatively low birth and death rates as a result of technological development.

_____ 5. The number of live births per 1000 people in a population in a given year.

_____ 6. The movement of people out of a geographic area to take up residency elsewhere.

_____ 7. The number of deaths per 1000 people in a population in a given year.

_____ 8. The movement of people into a geographic area to take up residency.

_____ 9. The incident of deaths in a population.

_____ 10. The number of deaths of infants under 1 year of age per 1000 live births in a given year.

_____ 11. A graphic representation of the distribution of a population by sex and age.

_____ 12. A subfield of sociology that examines social relationships and political and economic structures in the city.

_____ 13. The movement of people from one geographic area to another for the purpose of changing residency.

_____ 14. One or more central cities and their surrounding suburbs that dominate the economic and cultural life of a region.

_____ 15. The biological and social characteristics of a population.

_____ 16. The process by which a new category of people arrives in an area previously occupied by another group.

_____ 17. The process by which a new category of people or type of land use gradually predominates in an area formerly dominated by another group or activity.

_____ 18. The densely populated centre of a metropolis.

_____ 19. An estimate of the average lifetime in years of people born in a specific year.

Key People

Lynn M. Appleton (p. 488)

Paul Ehrlich and Anne H. Ehrlich (p. 478)

Herbert Gans (p. 490)

Chauncey Harris and Edward Ullman (p. 486)

Thomas Homer-Dixon (p. 480)

Homer Hoyt (p. 485)

Thomas Robert Malthus (p. 478)

Karl Marx and Friedrich Engels (p. 478)

Robert Park and
Ernest W. Burgess (p. 484)

Gideon Sjoberg (p. 482)

Georg Simmel (p. 488)

Louis Wirth (p. 488)

Review of Key People

_____ 1. Studied the configuration of 142 cities, and came up with a sector model that emphasizes the significance of terrain and the importance of transportation routes in the layout of cities.

_____ 2. Claimed that different cities have different ideas of how women and men should think, feel, and act; how access to social positions and control of resources should be managed; and how relationships between men and women should be conducted.

_____ 3. Suggested that the world was following an exponential growth pattern.

_____ 4. Developed a model in which cities have numerous centres of development based on specific urban needs or activities.

_____ 5. Claimed there are five major categories of adaptation among urban dwellers: cosmopolites, unmarried and childless couples, ethnic villagers, the deprived, and the trapped.

_____ 6. Believed that urban life was highly stimulating and shaped people's thoughts and actions.

_____ 7. Suggested that urbanization is a way of life.

_____ 8. Claimed that three preconditions must be necessary in order for a city to develop: a favourable physical environment, advanced technology, and a well-developed social organization.

_____ 9. Viewed poverty as a consequence of the exploitation of workers by the owners of the means of production.

_____ 10. Studied the relationship between people and their physical environment and developed the concentric zone model, which attempted to explain why some cities expand radically from a central business core.

_____ 11. Feels that increases in population and resource consumption will lead to significant environmental changes, including climatic instability and scarcities of soil and water.

_____ 12. Claimed that positive checks could avert the otherwise inevitability of world population growth surpassing the food supply.

Learning Objectives

After reading Chapter 15, the student should be able to:

1. define the study of demography and be able to identify key questions of interest to demographers (p. 463).

2. define fertility and explain how biological and social factors influence the level of fertility in a society (pp. 464-466).

3. define mortality and describe the two types of mortality rates demographers most often measure (pp. 466-468).

4. define migration and identify the two forms of movement (p. 468).

5. distinguish between internal and international migration and note the major causes of migration (pp. 468-471).

6. describe the impact of the baby boom and bust on Canadian society (pp. 473-477).

7. describe the key assumptions of the Marxist perspective on population growth and compare it to the Malthusian perspective (p. 478).

8. describe the neo-Malthusian perspective on population growth and note the significance of zero population growth to this perspective (pp. 478-480).

9. discuss demographic transition theory and be able to describe the four stages of economic development (pp. 480-481).

10. define urban sociology and note the proportion of Canada that is considered urban (p. 481).

11. trace the historical development of cities and identify the major characteristics of preindustrial, industrial, and postindustrial cities (pp. 482-484).

12. discuss functionalist perspectives on urbanization and outline the major ecological models of urban growth (pp. 484-487).

13. be able to define and distinguish between invasion and succession (p. 485).

14. outline conflict perspectives on urban growth (pp. 487-488).

15. explain interactionist perspectives on urban life and note the key assumptions of the major urban theorists (pp. 488-491).

16. discuss the major problems facing urban areas in Canada and the global population trends predicted for the 21st century (pp. 491-493).

Learning Objective Tests

Multiple Choice Questions

1. The movement of people from one geographic area to another for the purpose of changing residency is:
   a. migration.
   b. demographic transition.
   c. advanced industrialization.
   d. urbanization.

2. Which perspective re-emphasizes the dangers of overpopulation as a result of exponential growth patterns?
   a. Marxist
   b. neo-Marxist
   c. neo-Malthusian
   d. interactionist

3. Which of the following statements about demographic transition theory is TRUE?
    a. Very little population growth occurs in the advanced industrialization and urbanization stage due to low birth and death rates.
    b. Significant population growth occurs in preindustrial societies because birth rates remain very high while death rates decline.
    c. In postindustrialization, birth rates increase as the cost of raising children decreases.
    d. In the advanced industrialization and urbanization stage, children are viewed as economic assets.

4. Demographers are interested in all of the following questions EXCEPT:
    a. Why does the population grow rapidly in some nations?
    b. What are the consequences of low birth rate in industrialized countries?
    c. What effect might a widespread AIDS crisis have on world population?
    d. All of the above are questions of interest to demographers.

5. Which perspective views poverty and over population as a consequence of the exploitation of workers by the owners of the means of production?
    a. Mathusian
    b. Marxist
    c. neo-Marxist
    d. interactionist

6. All of the following factors affect fertility EXCEPT:
    a. the general health and level of nutrition of women of childbearing age.
    b. prevalent viewpoints regarding what constitutes the "ideal" family size.
    c. substantial increases in life expectancy.
    d. roles available to women in a society.

7. The primary cause of world population growth is:
    a. an increase in fertility.
    b. a decline in mortality.
    c. constant international migration.
    d. a diverse population composition.

8. What proportion of Canadian society is considered urban?
    a. 50 percent
    b. 60 percent
    c. 70 percent
    d. 80 percent

9. Gentrification is the process by which:
    a. members of the upper and middle classes move into the central city and renovate existing properties.
    b. a new category of people or type of land use arrives in an area previously occupied by another group or land use.
    c. a new category of people or type of land use gradually predominates in an area formerly dominated by another group or activity.
    d. some societies have moved from high birth rates and death rates to relatively low birth and death rates as a result of technological development.

10. According to Gideon Sjoberg (1963), this condition must be present for a city to develop.
    a. conflict among rural residents
    b. the capital to renovate existing properties
    c. a favourable physical environment, including soil favourable to plant and animal life
    d. good social planners who can construct adequate transportation routes throughout the city

11. For decades, people from the Atlantic provinces moved to Ontario in search of work. This illustrates:
    a. internal migration.
    b. international migration.
    c. demographic transition.
    d. urbanization.

12. The view that not everyone experiences life the same way and that personal characteristics can affect lifestyle choices is central to which perspective?
    a. conflict
    b. Mathusian
    c. interactionist
    d. structural functionalist

13. Functionalist (economic) models include all of the following EXCEPT:
    a. concentric zone.
    b. multiple nuclei.
    c. gender regimes.
    d. sector.

14. Which of the following statements about the baby boom and bust is FALSE?
    a. The baby boom was caused by young couples who married and began having children in the years immediately following World War II.
    b. Canadian families need to have fewer children in order to compensate for trends created by baby boomers.
    c. University enrollments and crime rates had begun to decline by the 1990s.
    d. The baby boomers have always constituted the largest age group in Canadian society.

15. _____ perspectives point out that urban patterns result from basic economic processes such as capital accumulation.
    a. Conflict
    b. Functionalist
    c. Interactionist
    d. Mathusian

16. Which of the following statements concerning population trends is FALSE?
    a. Mass urbanization in North America has created a territorial division of interests between cities and suburban areas.
    b. Starvation will be less and less of a problem in developing nations due to the economic aid of North America.
    c. Although death rates have declined in many developing nations, birth rates have not correspondingly decreased.
    d. HIV/AIDS may reach epidemic proportions as more nations and as many as 100 million AIDS cases may exist worldwide by the year 2000.

True–False Statements

TF   1. The world's population is decreasing by 94 million people per year (p. 462).

TF   2. Fertility rates are equal to fecundity rates (p. 465).

TF   3. Underdeveloped countries with high birth rates also have high infant mortality rates (p. 467).

TF   4. Migration affects the size and distribution of a population in a given area (p. 468).

TF   5. Immigration is the movement of people out of a geographic area to take up residence elsewhere (p. 468).

TF   6. The baby boom and bust has had very little impact on the age structure of Canadian society (p. 474).

TF   7.   Canada's fertility is now 2.1 children per woman, which will provide replacement of our population (p. 477).

TF   8.   According to the Marxist perspective, it is possible to produce the food and other goods needed to meet the demands of a growing population (p. 478).

TF   9.   Invasion is the process by which a new category of people gradually predominates in an area formerly dominated by another group (p. 485).

TF   10. The strength of our urban core is a major reason Canadian cities have much lower crime rates than American cities (p. 487).

Fill-in-the-Blanks

1.   Demographers define _____ as a group of people who live in a specified geographical area (p. 464).

2.   _____ is the potentional number of children that could be born if every woman reproduced at her maximum biological capacity (p. 465).

3.   The most basic measure of fertility is the _____ _____ _____, the number of live births per 1000 people in a population in a given year (p. 466).

4.   Our declining mortality rates have led to substantial increases in _____ _____, which is an estimate of the average lifetime in years of people born in a specific year (p. 468).

5.   A _____ is one or more central cities and their surrounding suburbs that dominate the economic and cultural life of a region (p. 483).

6.   According to the _____ _____ _____ developed by urban ecologists Harris and Ullman (1945), cities do not have one centre from which all growth radiates but, rather, they have numerous centres of development (p. 486).

7.   _____ theorists argue that cities do not grow or decline by chance; rather, they are the product of specific decisions made by members of the capitalist class (p. 487).

8.   _____ examine the experience of urban life, including how the city life affects the people who live in the city (p. 488).

9.   According to Herbert Gans, _____ are students, artists, writers, musicians, entertainers, and professionals who live in the city because they want to be close to its cultural facilities (p. 490).

10.   By 2010, Rio de Janeiro and Sao Paulo are expected to have a combined population of about 40 million people living in a 350-mile-long _____ (p. 492).

Matching Items

1. Match the central feature to its corresponding ecological model.

___ (a) invasion and succession   1. concentric zone model
___ (b) terrain and transportation   2. sector model
___ (c) many centres of development   3. multiple nuclei model

2. Match the characteristic with the appropriate theoretical perspective.

___ (a) concentric zone model   1. functionalist perspective
___ (b) gender regimes in cities   2. conflict perspective
___ (c) urbanism as a way of life   3. interactionist perspective

ANSWERS TO LEARNING OBJECTIVE TESTS

Chapter 1

Multiple Choice Items:

1. b	(learning objective 4)	11. b	(learning objective 8)
2. a	(learning objective 5)	12. a	(learning objective 14)
3. a	(learning objective 1)	13. b	(learning objective 12)
4. d	(learning objective 11)	14. a	(learning objective 13)
5. c	(learning objective 9)	15. c	(learning objective 15)
6. d	(learning objective 2)	16. b	(learning objective 19)
7. a	(learning objective 3)	17. c	(learning objective 17)
8. d	(learning objective 6)	18. c	(learning objective 18)
9. b	(learning objective 7)	19. b	(learning objective 20)
10. d	(learning objective 107)	20. d	(learning objective 16)

True–False Statements:
1. T
2. F
3. F
4. T
5. F
6. T
7. F
8. T
9. T
10. F

Fill-in-the-Blanks:
1. sociology
2. conflict
3. power; prestige
4. societal consensus
5. sociological imagination
6. macrolevel
7. ethnography
8. empirical approach
9. correlation
10. representative sample

Matching:
1. concepts and theoretical perspectives: 2, 1, 3
2. concepts with originators: 3, 2, 1
3. method with form of data collection: 2, 1, 3, 4

Chapter 2

Multiple Choice Items:

1. d	(learning objective 4)	9. c	(learning objective 2)
2. a	(learning objective 6)	10. c	(learning objective 12)
3. b	(learning objective 7)	11. b	(learning objective 16)
4. d	(learning objective 3)	12. d	(learning objective 10)
5. c	(learning objective 1)	13. b	(learning objective 14)
6. d	(learning objective 9)	14. c	(learning objective 15)
7. a	(learning objective 11)	15. a	(learning objective 13)
8. d	(learning objective 5)	16. a	(learning objective 8)

True–False Statements:
1. T
2. T
3. F
4. T
5. T

Fill-in-the-Blanks:
1. value
2. nonmaterial culture
3. symbol
4. language

Matching:
1. example and type of norm: 2, 1, 3
2. statement with perspective: 1, 3, 2

Chapter 3

Multiple Choice Items:

1. b	(learning objective 6)	9. c	(learning objective 4)
2. a	(learning objective 7)	10. b	(learning objective 5)
3. d	(learning objective 10)	11. b	(learning objective 14)
4. a	(learning objective 12)	12. c	(learning objective 8)
5. c	(learning objective 1)	13. c	(learning objective 13)
6. d	(learning objective 3)	14. d	(learning objective 11)
7. b	(learning objective 9)	15. d	(learning objective 15)
8. d	(learning objective 2)		

True–False Statements:
1. T
2. T
3. F
4. T
5. F
6. T
7. F
8. T
9. T
10. T

Fill-in-the-Blanks:
1. agents of socialization
2. looking-glass self
3. preparatory stage
4. socialization
5. workplace or occupational
6. peer groups
7. mass media
8. id
9. role-taking
10. self-identity

Matching:
1. concept with theorist: 2, 1, 5, 3, 4

Chapter 4

Multiple Choice Items:

1. d	(learning objective 4)	9. c	(learning objective 5)
2. a	(learning objective 2)	10. a	(learning objective 6)
3. b	(learning objective 9)	11. c	(learning objective 8)
4. d	(learning objective 7)	12. d	(learning objective 10)
5. b	(learning objective 11)	13. c	(learning objective 16)
6. a	(learning objective 12)	14. d	(learning objective 13)
7. c	(learning objective 3)	15. d	(learning objective 15)
8. b	(learning objective 1)	16. a	(learning objective 14)

17. c	(learning objective 17)	22. b	(learning objective 22)
18. d	(learning objective 18)	23. d	(learning objective 23
19. b	(learning objective 20)	24. b	(learning objective 25)
20. b	(learning objective 19)	25. b	(learning objective 24)
21. a	(learning objective 21)		

True–False Statements:

1. T	10. T	
2. T	11. T	
3. F	12. F	
4. F	13. T	
5. T	14. F	
6. T	15. T	
7. T	16. T	
8. F	17. T	
9. T		

Fill-in-the-Blanks:

1. occupy; play	9. institutions
2. social structure	10. conventional crowds
3. status set	11. acting
4. master status	12. civil disobedience
5. status symbol	13. emergent norm theory
6. role ambiguity	14. gossip
7. primary group	15. revolutionary
8. formal organizations	16. alternative

Matching:
1. concept with crowd type: 2, 1, 3, 4, 5
2. concept with theory on collective behaviour: 2, 1, 3

Chapter 5

Multiple Choice Items:

1. c	(learning objective 3)	9. c	(learning objective 6)
2. d	(learning objective 2)	10. b	(learning objective 4)
3. c	(learning objective 9)	11. b	(learning objective 10)
4. d	(learning objective 8)	12. d	(learning objective 11)
5. b	(learning objective 1)	13. d	(learning objective 13)
6. b	(learning objective 5)	14. d	(learning objective 14)
7. c	(learning objective 7)	15. a	(learning objective 15)
8. c	(learning objective 12)		

True–False Statements:

1. T
2. F
3. F
4. T
5. T

Fill-in-the-Blanks:

1. aggregates
2. ingroup;outgroup
3. dyad
4. authoritarian
5. utilitarian

Matching:
1. leadership style with group characteristic: 2, 1, 3

Chapter 6

Multiple Choice Items:

1. c	(learning objective 7)	10. a	(learning objective 5)
2. d	(learning objective 8)	11. a	(learning objective 11)
3. b	(learning objective 3)	12. d	(learning objective 13)
4. c	(learning objective 2)	13. b	(learning objective 12)
5. c	(learning objective 9)	14. a	(learning objective 18)
6. b	(learning objective 6)	15. d	(learning objective 15)
7. d	(learning objective 1)	16. c	(learning objective 17)
8. c	(learning objective 10)	17. d	(learning objective 16)
9. d	(learning objective 4)	18. a	(learning objective 14)

True–False Statements:
1. T
2. T
3. F
4. T
5. F
6. T
7. F
8. F
9. T
10. F

Fill-in-the-Blanks:
1. criminal justice system
2. deterrence
3. Canadian Uniform Crime Reports
4. organized crime
5. labelling
6. attachment, commitment, involvement, belief
7. social control
8. illegitimate opportunity structures
9. goals; means

Matching:
1. theories to perspectives: 2, 1, 3

Chapter 7

Multiple Choice Items:

1. d	(learning objective 3)	10. d	(learning objective 13)
2. b	(learning objective 1)	11. a	(learning objective 17)
3. d	(learning objective 6)	12. a	(learning objective 10)
4. b	(learning objective 14)	13. c	(learning objective 5)
5. d	(learning objective 16)	14. d	(learning objective 7)
6. a	(learning objective 4)	15. d	(learning objective 11)
7. c	(learning objective 9)	16. d	(learning objective 15)
8. b	(learning objective 2)	17. a	(learning objective 8)
9. b	(learning objective 12)		

True–False Statements:

1. F	6. T
2. T	7. F
3. F	8. T
4. F	9. T
5. T	

Fill-in-the-Blanks:

1. caste	6. conflict
2. Power	7. income
3. Davis-Moore	8. wealth
4. Prestige	9. job deskilling
5. Power	

Matching:
1. Match the theorist with the appropriate concept: 2, 3, 1

Chapter 8

Multiple Choice Items:

1. c	(learning objective 16)	11. d	(learning objective 13)
2. a	(learning objective 14	12. c	(learning objective 15)
3. d	(learning objective 19)	13. b	(learning objective 5)
4. b	(learning objective 3)	14. d	(learning objective 4)
5. a	(learning objective 6)	15. b	(learning objective 8)
6. b	(learning objective 17)	16. b	(learning objective 10)
7. b	(learning objective 1)	17. d	(learning objective 20)
8. d	(learning objective 2)	18. c	(learning objective 12)
9. d	(learning objective 9)	19. b	(learning objective 11)
10. a	(learning objective 18)	20. a	(learning objective 7)

True–False Statements:

1. F
2. T
3. F
4. T
5. T
6. T
7. T
8. F
9. F
10. T

Fill-in-the-Blanks:

1. white privilege
2. visible minority
3. ethnocentrism
4. systemic
5. upper tier
6. cultural assimilation
7. structural assimilation
8. segregation

Matching:

1. theory with its key assumption: 4, 2, 1, 3
2. pattern of interaction with feature: 5, 1, 3, 2, 4

Chapter 9

Multiple Choice Items:

1. c	(learning objective 2)	10. a	(learning objective 3
2. d	(learning objective 6)	11. d	(learning objective 5)
3. a	(learning objective 9)	12. d	(learning objective 8)
4. d	(learning objective 10)	13. b	(learning objective 17)
5. d	(learning objective 12)	14. c	(learning objective 15)
6. c	(learning objective 13)	15. a	(learning objective 14)
7. d	(learning objective 16)	16. c	(learning objective 7)
8. c	(learning objective 18)	17. c	(learning objective 4)
9. b	(learning objective 1)	18. c	(learning objective 11)

True–False Statements:

1. F
2. T
3. T
4. T
5. F

Fill-in-the-Blanks:

1. secondary sex characteristics
2. hermaphrodites
3. transexual
4. gendered institutions
5. pay equity

6. T
7. F
8. T
9. T
10. T

6. gender role
7. sex
8. employment equity
9. functionalist
10. radical

Matching:
1. society with key feature: 2, 1, 3, 4
2. socialization agent and key characteristic: 3, 4, 1, 2, 5
3. theoretical perspective and key argument: 3, 1, 2, 5, 6, 4

Chapter 10

Multiple Choice Items:

1. a	(learning objective 5)	6. d	(learning objective 2)
2. d	(learning objective 6)	7. d	(learning objective 7)
3. c	(learning objective 1)	8. a	(learning objective 8
4. a	(learning objective 3)	9. d	(learning objective 10)
5. b	(learning objective 4)	10. d	(learning objective 9)

True–False Statements:
1. T
2. F
3. T
4. T
5. F

Fill-in-the-Blanks:
1. medicalization
2. disability oppression
3. universal health care
4. accessibility
5. holism

Chapter 11

Multiple Choice Items:

1. b	(learning objective 2)	8. d	(learning objective 14)
2. b	(learning objective 5)	9. b	(learning objective 12)
3. c	(learning objective 9)	10. a	(learning objective 4)
4. c	(learning objective 13)	11. d	(learning objective 3)
5. d	(learning objective 1)	12. a	(learning objective 7)
6. d	(learning objective 8)	13. c	(learning objective 6)
7. b	(learning objective 10)	14. b	(learning objective 11)

True–False Statements:
1. F
2. F
3. T
4. T
5. T
6. F
7. F
8. T

Fill-in-the-Blanks:
1. services
2. labour
3. capital
4. tertiary sector production
5. competition
6. democratic socialism
7. job satisfaction

Matching:
1. economy to it key charactistic: 3, 2, 1
2. economic system to its corresponding feature: 3, 1, 2

Chapter 12

Multiple Choice Items:

1. a	(learning objective 5)	8. c	(learning objective 3)
2. d	(learning objective 8)	9. b	(learning objective 7)
3. c	(learning objective 1)	10. c	(learning objective 12)
4. b	(learning objective 4)	11. b	(learning objective 2)
5. d	(learning objective 10)	12. b	(learning objective 9)
6. a	(learning objective 6)	13. c	(learning objective 13)
7. d	(learning objective 11)		

True–False Statements:
1. F
2. F
3. F
4. T
5. T

Fill-in-the-Blanks:
1. government
2. power
3. legitimation
4. charismatic
5. rational-legal authority
6. Charter; Rights, Freedoms
7. totalitarianism
8. liberal

Matching:
1. political system with main characteristic: 3, 4, 1, 2
2. authority with key feature: 1, 3, 2

Chapter 13

Multiple Choice Items:

1. b	(learning objective 6)	10. b	(learning objective 8)
2. b	(learning objective 2)	11. d	(learning objective 18)
3. c	(learning objective 9)	12. a	(learning objective 10)
4. d	(learning objective 14)	13. a	(learning objective 7)
5. c	(learning objective 12)	14. c	(learning objective 13)
6. c	(learning objective 15)	15. d	(learning objective 11)
7. d	(learning objective 17)	16. a	(learning objective 3)
8. c	(learning objective 5)	17. d	(learning objective 1)
9. c	(learning objective 4)	18. d	(learning objective 16)

True–False Statements:

1. F	7. T
2. F	8. T
3. T	9. T
4. F	10. T
5. F	
6. T	

Fill-in-the-Blanks:
1. family of procreation
2. nuclear
3. monogamy
4. polygyny
5. sociology; family
6. blended

Matching:
1. marriage pattern to marriage characteristic: 1, 3, 2
2. residential pattern to key characteristic: 3, 2, 1

Chapter 14

Multiple Choice Items:

1. d	(learning objective 8)	8. a	(learning objective 6)
2. d	(learning objective 2)	9. a	(learning objective 10)
3. a	(learning objective 11)	10. b	(learning objective 9)
4. a	(learning objective 12)	11. b	(learning objective 5)
5. b	(learning objective 4)	12. d	(learning objective 13)
6. c	(learning objective 7)	13. c	(learning objective 2)
7. d	(learning objective 3)		

True–False Statements:
1. T
2. F
3. T
4. F
5. T
6. T

Fill-in-the-Blanks:
1. culture capital
2. hidden curriculum
3. rituals
4. ecclesia
5. denomination

Matching:
1. concept with appropriate perspective on education: 1, 2, 3

Chapter 15

Multiple Choice Items:

1. a	(learning objective 4)	9. a	(learning objective 13)
2. c	(learning objective 8)	10. c	(learning objective 11)
3. a	(learning objective 9)	11. a	(learning objective 5)
4. d	(learning objective 1)	12. c	(learning objective 15)
5. b	(learning objective 7)	13. c	(learning objective 12)
6. c	(learning objective 2)	14. b	(learning objective 6)
7. b	(learning objective 3)	15. a	(learning objective 14)
8. d	(learning objective 10)	16. b	(learning objective 16)

True–False Statements:

1. F	6. F
2. F	7. F
3. T	8. T
4. T	9. F
5. F	10. T

Fill-in-the-Blanks:

1. Population	6. multiple nuclei model
2. Fecundity	7. conflict
3. crude birth rate	8. interactionists
4. life expectancy	9. cosmopolites
5. Metropolis	10. megalopolis

Matching:
1. central feature to ecological model: 1, 2, 3
2. characteristic with theoretical perspective: 1, 2, 3